Living
Change

*the power of change to
transform your life*

a workplace story of an INPowering life by
Garland C. McWatters

episode 4

A workplace story of an INPowering Life
The series (so far)

Confronting Your Moment of Truth
a Quest for Clarity
a New Way to Lead
Living Change

Published by INPowered to LEAD Inc. Tulsa, OK
contact: information@inpoweredtolead.com
972/762-3955

ISBN-13: 978-1720438434
ISBN-10: 1720438439
Printed by CreateSpace, An Amazon.com Company
Available from Amazon.com, CreateSpace.com, and other retail outlets

For my grandchildren,
who will change the world.

"Just when the
caterpillar thought
the world was over,
it became
a butterfly."

Chuang Tzu

Preface

The INPowered life is one in which a person takes charge of his or her circumstances and makes the most of them. An INPowering person is one who helps others find strength from the reservoir of their own creative energy. I believe everyone aspires to live with that type of control over his or her destiny.

The INPowered are not easily thrown off by change. Although there are no pat answers for dealing with change, the INPowered find a way to understand and work through inevitable changes that are an innate part of living. Still, even for the most resilient, change can be complex and difficult, even emotionally devastating. Each individual experiences change differently. A positive change for one might be disruptive for another and vice versa.

This episode, *Living Change*, is timely for Marcus's ongoing Workplace Story of an INPowering Life. The first three episodes presented a young new supervisor who had to confront some inconvenient truths about his job status and performance. Marcus Winn faced changes and opportunities he did not expect. This episode reflects on some of those changes and brings Marcus to a time when those changes begin to intensify for him, his friends, and colleagues. They represent evolutionary, revolutionary, and transformational changes that will shape Marcus's future.

I have placed some background information on the dynamics of change at the conclusion of this episode. My intent is to help you discuss the various stories of change you will encounter presented from a variety of perspectives in the story line. They are at the back in case you want to enjoy the story first, before jumping into a more reflective study and discussion of what happened. Or, you can read that section first. It's up to you.

I hope you will find much food for thought and discussion. I hope the stories of change that you encounter will help you find insights into how you can become more IN-Powered to take advantage of the possibilities that come from living change.

Garland McWatters

Contents

Living Change

1. Dizzying heights

Change, even good change, can be disorienting. Marcus Winn felt like he was tumbling in some kind of an emotional vertigo. He needed to find something to grab hold of to right himself.

The spinning started seven months ago. Marcus remembered sitting head-in-hands on a lakeside bench near his sister's home, distraught over whether he could figure out how to save his job as a recently promoted supervisor of an obscure project team. Today, here he stood, a company-wide celebrity, on the edge of the expansive patio of his CEO's daughter's palatial home overlooking Lake Dohi, northeast of Tulsa. *Is this real? Somebody please pinch me,* Marcus thought.

Lizzie Frisk was a fan. She was in the audience with her dad, Nelson Johnstone, three week earlier at the Johnstone Energy Enterprises leadership retreat when Marcus spoke about leading his project team through some challenging successes in recent months. He was totally unprepared for how dramatically that one presentation would change his life. A good change, but disorienting none-the-less.

Lizzie made a bee line to meet him after his talk. Later that evening she invited him to this Memorial Day weekend cookout. Marcus remembered his first thought was to call his girlfriend, AnnaMarie Flores, and invite her down from Springfield for the weekend as his plus one.

The vista surrounding Lake Dohi lived up to the lake's Cherokee name, meaning tranquil. Just standing there quietly with the May breeze brushing his face relaxed Marcus as he tried to release the disappointment he felt from Anna's call last evening when she unexpectedly canceled her plans to the cookout. Work commitments, again.

Back in October I was just hoping I could hold onto my promotion after Erin called me in and told me I wasn't living up to her expectations. I felt like I was going to collapse from the inside out. I couldn't bear the humiliation of a demotion. I don't know how I would have handled losing my job entirely. All the worst-case scenarios trashed my thoughts. I left work confused and pissed without a clue why all that was happening to me or how I was going to turn Erin around. I felt like everything I had worked for was being ripped away, and I had been working so hard to do a good job.

Then I met AnnaMarie at a Springfield soccer field, coaching my nephew, Andy. She blew me away. I wanted her the instant I saw her. That same weekend I met Jeannie Irwin sitting beside the lake near my sister's home crying her eyes out. She was thinking about running away from home because of how her mother and stepdad treated her. Both of these women have come to mean so much to me, each in her way. If it were not for both of them that weekend, I'm not sure I would have figured out how to get myself together. I've never told them that—that they showed me how I could fix things with Erin.

I thought Anna would be the woman I'd make a life with, and that somehow we would work out the distance relationship issues. I know her job demands most of her time. I've heard stories about the work schedule of new lawyers. Now I get it. But we had weekends together, usually in Springfield and sometimes here in Tulsa. I was happy taking what I could get. I've always thought it would get better.

Until Eric Greer entered the picture. Rich, a successful businessman, charming, charismatic–according to Anna– and, now, running for Congress. And single. Well, actually engaged, but that can change in a flash. Now he wants Anna on his legal team, and since he's a major client, Eric gets what Eric wants.

She told me she was ninety-nine percent sure she could be here today. Then, Greer surprised his campaign committee yesterday, saying he needed to have all-hands-on-deck for a fund raising event today.

The thing about the call was that Anna sounded more excited about Greer's event than she was disappointed about not making it to the cookout. I can feel Anna slipping away, and I don't know how to stop it. Damn you, Eric Greer.

"Hey, Marcus, why're you standin' over here all alone like?" Lizzie strolled up from behind and stood beside Marcus, taking in the panorama. "Beautiful view, isn't it?"

Change, even good change can be disorienting.

"Spectacular. Almost hypnotic," Marcus did not break his gaze that stretched miles over the tops of the rolling wooded hills that still hid the new neighborhoods cropping up on sections of inherited family farms and ranches sold off to developers by heirs with appetites for huge profits.

"Yeah, I know," Lizzie folded her arms, gazing across the southern vista. "You should see it when a thunderhead is buildin' in the southwest. Sometimes I'll sit out here and watch it 'til the storm chases me inside." Lizzie paused. Marcus stood entranced. "Then there's nothin' sweeter than smellin' the air when the storm passes. Everything is all fresh again. Changed. Recharged."

Lizzie's Okie drawl added that farm girl charm to a woman who exuded a determined confidence wrapped in country casualness. The unmistakable family resemblance with her father showed in her modelesque five-foot, ten-inch frame, oval face, and deep-set brown eyes. Today, she parted her light blonde hair in the middle, allowing it to drape gently over her round tanned shoulders and back. She moved with an elegant flow that could have easily graced a New York fashion runway.

Marcus broke the spontaneous silence, "I've been fascinated by storms since I was a boy," His gaze held southward. "That's why I got into wind energy. How can I take all that natural energy that can destroy so much so quickly, like in Moore again last week, and do something positive with it? Someday I'm going to figure out how to use it to power a city like Tulsa, or maybe Dallas."

"You sound like my dad when he talks about the oil business," Lizzie turned to face Marcus. "Your passion comes through. Just like it did in your speech at the leadership retreat."

"No one was more surprised by the reaction than me," Marcus chuckled.

"I hear the video of your speech is gettin' a lot of play on the company website."

"Yeah, I'm actually a little self-conscious about that. I was OK with being just another face in the crowd around campus. Now, just about everyone recognizes me. It's a very awkward feeling. All this change is a bit overwhelming."

"Marcus, I'm sorry your girlfriend couldn't make it at the last minute. We were lookin' forward to meetin' her." Lizzie pivoted and took Marcus's arm in hers and guided him back across the patio toward the house and the other guests.

"Me, too. I'm sure she would have enjoyed being here," Marcus dropped his gaze as they sauntered. "She's the newest associate in her firm. One of her clients has turned into a politician and had her assigned to his campaign. That's her priority right now."

"Sounds like you're workin' through some new relationship stuff."

"Yeah. Trying to figure out all these changes."

"But on the up side," Lizzie perked up her tone, "your last-minute stand in is delightful. Does Theresa ever meet a stranger?" Lizzie stopped with Marcus still in arm, and glanced over to a group of two other couples and Theresa in the middle of them, circled up, laughing hysterically.

"Probably not. She sure has introduced me to a lot of people around the campus. I think I've become her latest social project." Marcus smiled as Lizzie released his arm.

"Well, I'm glad she was available. I better tend to my other guests. I was goin' to introduce you around, but it looks like Theresa might be able to take it from here. I'm eager for my friends to meet you. I think they'll take to you the way I have and will be good contacts for an up-and-comer like you."

"Up-and-comer?" Marcus hesitated. "I'm not sure I'd call myself that."

"Sure you are, Marcus, honey," Lizzie looked Marcus squarely in the eyes and smiled, squeezing his forearm. "I'll check on you in a bit."

"There you are, Marcus," Theresa spied Marcus coming toward her and waived for him to join in. "Come over here and let me introduce you." She reached and took Marcus's left hand as he approached and held it. "This is Eva and Neal McDaniel." Each offered Marcus their hand. Theresa continued to hold on to Marcus. "And this is Alexis and Pete Olson."

"A pleasure to meet you," Marcus nodded.

"Marcus, you've obviously made quite an impression on Lizzie," Pete said. "She shared the video of your speech from the retreat with me. And Theresa, here, is without question the president of your fan club. How long have you two been together?"

"Oh, well . . . er," Marcus stammered, "We're n–," Theresa squeezed his hand, and he looked into her face, "I mean, we, uh . . . we met in February," Marcus looked back at Pete. Marcus changed the subject, "How are you all connected with the Frisks?"

"Actually, through Travis," Neal responded. "We go way back with Travis to his early days in Tulsa when he was just starting out. We've been friends and done business together. I have a specialty precision machining business, and Travis uses me for some of his aviation projects."

"And we raised families together," Eva interrupted.

"And played a lot of golf," Neal added. Everyone laughed. "You a golfer, Marcus?"

"I'm more into running. I ran cross country in high school and college. I've been training to do some road races coming up."

"It's been an amazing life together," Alexis joined in. "The thing about Lizzie is how down to earth she is. If you just met her on the street you wouldn't know she's from one of the wealthiest families in the world."

"I know Johnstone Energy is a successful super independent oil company," Marcus said.

"And the oil company is the tip of the iceberg," Neal went on. "It's the enterprises part that will blow your mind. Forbes has him in the top 50 worldwide."

"He's also made a lot of other people rich," Pete added. "You just never hear him talk about it."

"And you won't," Alexis interrupted. "Nelson is quiet about his wealth. Humble, as a matter of fact. And I don't know anyone who works harder than Lizzie at being a philanthropist."

"She takes after her dad that way," Eva said. "They are so approachable and kind."

"Ya'll talkin' about me? My ears are burnin'," Lizzie walked up, splitting Eva and Alexis in the circle, draping her arms over each of their shoulders. "Travis just called and said he is about five minutes out. On final approach as he calls it. Sends his apologies for bein' late . . . again. Oh, heck, everyone knows Travis is ten minutes behind everyone else." Everyone laughed in agreement. Lizzie looked at Theresa standing opposite her in the circle, "Theresa, you look familiar, and I've been tryin' to place where I've seen you ever since you all got here."

"I attended a fund raiser you helped organize last

year at the Gilcrease," Theresa answered.

"I can't imagine you didn't introduce yourself."

"You were busy, and I was a bit taken by the art there."

"Well, now we're friends. And you must be pretty good friends with Marcus for him to invite you at the last minute, and for you to drop everythin' and come." Lizzie noticed Theresa had a grip on Marcus's hand, and that Marcus didn't seem to be resisting.

"I think he's pretty special," Theresa glanced admiringly up at Marcus, causing him to cast a shy glance at the floor. "I'm just lucky to get the chance to be here and to meet so many interesting people. And your home is fabulous."

Lizzie noticed Marcus blushing, "Well, when Travis gets here I'll bring him around. Everyone else here already knows him." With that, Lizzie noticed some new arrivals, "Excuse me, the Jenkins just got here," and she disappeared across the patio.

"Well, you two," Alexis addressed both Marcus and Theresa, "Since you're the newest to the group, how about Eva and I make sure you meet everyone?"

"I'll catch up with you later," Pete saluted Marcus with his beer bottle, "I'd like to hear more about how you came by your leadership ideas."

"Sure thing, Pete," Marcus replied.

Theresa's face beamed, glancing up at Marcus. She released his hand, reluctantly.

As much as Marcus had wanted AnnaMarie to be with him today, Theresa Younger slipped easily into the role of party companion. She had a social ease about her that naturally attracted others. She made him feel more comfortable among a class of successful and connected couples who made up Tulsa's emerging business elite. Whether it was as a colleague at Johnstone Energy, or at Jazzy Jake's club—a favorite nightspot where Marcus sometimes met Theresa and her friends, or at Lizzie Frisk's patio cookout, Theresa effortlessly connected with any and all. Marcus admired that.

The diversity of the Frisk's inner circle impressed Marcus as Alexis and Eva introduced him and Theresa. Although they were the youngest couple at the cookout, everyone made them feel welcome. The one thing every couple had in common, as he discovered, was that Lizzie had shared the video of his leadership retreat speech and insisted they watch it. These were the Frisk's closest friends, and he was among them.

"Marcus, it looks like you and Theresa are fittin' right in," Lizzie walked up with Travis in tow. "I finally got Travis off his phone and out of his office upstairs." Lizzie led him up to the group. "Travis, this is Marcus Winn, the young man I've been tellin' you about, and his friend Theresa Younger. Theresa works for Daddy, too. Marcus, Theresa, this is my husband, Travis."

Travis extended his hand, "My pleasure, Marcus," then to Theresa, "You, too Theresa. I apologize for being late to my own party. The nature of the aviation business."

Travis still carried his fighter pilot confidence in his walk and posture. "You know, Marcus, I got leadership training pounded into me both at the academy and as part of my officer training in the field," Travis said. "I'll have to admit I was fascinated by the simplicity and relevance of your message to JE's management. I understand from Lizzie that the company is building a training program around your ideas. That's quite an accomplishment."

That awkward shyness in Marcus resurged, "Well, I was surprised by the reaction. All I wanted to do was be the kind of supervisor that my project manager thought I could be. A week before the retreat, I didn't know for sure what I was going to say," Marcus admitted, shaking his head.

Lizzie spoke to Travis, "Marcy coached him."

"She's the best," Travis agreed. "Marcy is a dear friend." He looked at Theresa, "So, how are you two connected?"

Theresa answered quickly, "Just great friends. You might call me his wingman at work."

"That would be a fair way to put it," Marcus grinned, fully relaxing for the first time since arriving.

"Theresa, how'd you like to see some of the art I have hangin' in the house?" Lizzie asked.

"I'd be thrilled," Theresa let Lizzie take her arm.

Travis turned to Marcus, "In the meantime, let me take you around for some guy talk. I understand you are an OSU grad."

"Yes sir."

"Just Travis. OK? And you're going to fit right in with this crowd."

This is the kind of change I can get used to, Marcus thought.

* * *

Theresa rode quietly, eyes straight ahead with an occasional glance out her passenger window, as Marcus drove in silence toward her modest home in Maple Ridsge, an established Tulsa neighborhood. Nearly half an hour had passed since turning south onto highway 169 after leaving the Frisk's estate.

Marcus stared blankly ahead. His 370Z whizzed past

the joggers dotting the trail along Riverside Drive. Young mothers, striving to stay fit, ran pushing jogging strollers. Couples walked dogs that would rather sniff leisurely along the edges of the sidewalk than walk obediently on the leash. Others–both men and women–jogged behind their dogs that had figured out how to match their master's pace. Mostly, though, people were out for an evening stroll and getting the feel of the first official weekend of the summer season.

Theresa's neighborhood was coming up. Marcus had been there a couple of weeks earlier when he accepted an invitation to a home cooked dinner to celebrate his successful speech at the retreat. Theresa told him of the elderly couple, the Davenports, who had shared a life together in that home. They were now in a retirement community, and she felt lucky to have been in the right place at the right time to grab it up as a rental. Everything changes, and life goes on.

"You've been quiet since we left the Frisk's," Theresa broke the silence. "I hope I didn't do anything that offended you or made you feel uncomfortable."

"No . . . You didn't . . .To the contrary." Marcus cocked his head slightly to the right and glanced at Theresa out of the corner of his eyes, breaking into a shy grin. "Just thinking. That's all."

"Good, I know I shouldn't have held your hand like that. You know, when Pete asked us how long we had been together . . .I just really felt connected to you, and I didn't want to let go," Theresa turned and looked at Marcus.

Marcus glanced at Theresa and flashed a slight smile, "When you described yourself as my wingman, it made me think about the way we met and where we are now."

"Yeah, about that . . . I was a little . . . uh, forward, wasn't I?"

"A little?" Marcus laughed out loud. "I was dumbfounded. After all, it was Valentine's Day."

"Like I said, I wanted to know where I stood, if you were already taken. I might have been a little pushy," Theresa paused looking over to Marcus, grinning. "If the door of opportunity was cracked, I wanted to push it a little more open and see what happened."

"More like you ran through it . . . and knocked it off the hinges."

"Yeah, maybe, but when an opportunity presents itself, I don't often stand around wondering whether to take action. I go with it, and what happens, happens. And besides, it was Valentine's Day."

"Ha-ha-ha," a spontaneous laugh exploded from Marcus. "I'm actually glad you did . . . When you walked away I watched you until you turned the corner to the elevators."

"I know."

"How? You never looked back."

"Girls just know things."

"How? I never gave you any indication. In fact, if I remember correctly, I told you I was seeing someone and that I thought you were getting a little personal."

"That you did. But you couldn't see what I saw."

"And what was that?"

"Your eyes."

Marcus refocused on the road, "Better pay attention to where I'm going. Wouldn't want to miss the turn."

Theresa let the moment sink in.

"So, did you have other plans tonight?" Marcus asked, turning down her street.

"Meeting some of my friends at Jazzy Jake's at eight."

"Do I know any of them?"

"Not yet. But you could by the time you bring me home later tonight. Unless you're too busy."

"Busy, I am not, as it turns out," Marcus replied.

"So pick me up at 7:30?" Theresa smiled.

"It's a date," Marcus felt lightheaded as soon as he said it.

"That it is," Theresa grinned mischievously.

2. New Connections

Sunday morning was supposed to have been brunch with Anna, but now Marcus had no immediate plans. Marcus flipped through the calendar on his phone. He high-lighted the bar that read "Anna Here," and pressed the delete key. *I wonder what Anna's doing. I wonder if she will try to call today? Should I call her? . . . No. She's the one who changed all the plans for the weekend. I'm not going to chase her around begging for her time and attention. Maybe I'll go for a run. Don't want to let myself go, especially when I've made so much progress getting back into shape. Just look at you, Marcus. Been years since you've had this physique.*

Another set of highlighted dates caught his attention. He reserved the second week of June to go with Jim Bob Danner, a drilling engineer with Johnstone Oil and Gas, to visit several well sites in Montana. Marcus was nervous about the trip. He didn't know if he would like being around Jim Bob. They certainly had not gotten off on the right foot when, the first time they met in April, Jim Bob called him, "a pretty boy full of hot air," to his face.

I don't know what got into me to reach out to Jim Bob after he insulted me, but somehow it seemed like I should take the first step to make our relationship better. Everyone says he's a great drilling engineer and has some redeeming qualities. I can't imagine what they might be, but what the hell. I'm sure I can learn something, and I am curious about what it's like to be on a rig.

Maybe I'll give Theresa a call. Marcus started to dial her number. *Hold on. Better not go there.*

A hint of Theresa's fragrance lingered. Probably because of her extended embrace and kiss on the cheek marking the end of their so-called date just after midnight when Marcus walked her to her front door. *I'm glad I didn't let that go any farther. I don't want our friendship to get complicated or awkward. And besides, there's Anna.*

His phone pinged that a new message had come in. It was from Jeannie. "good morning. bet u had a blast at the party yesterday. camera is fantastic! u blew me away when I opened the box. here are some of the first pix I made. no photoshopping. hope u and Anna enjoy them. come c me soon."

Seems like a month since I saw Anna, but it was only last week for Jeannie's graduation. Boy, Jeannie was so surprised to get my graduation gift. It might have been a little over the top, but it's not every day you graduate from high school. An HD camera seemed like the perfect gift to me, with Jeannie taking photography classes this fall and starting college. I had the money.

But the best gift of all was Jeannie's dad surprising her when he came in from Chicago the day before. Jeannie was deliriously happy. The first time in two years that she'd seen him. Her own mother barely showed for the graduation ceremony and seemed like she couldn't wait to get away to finish packing for a cruise she and Nick went on this week. What a piece of work those two are. But again, Lauren to the rescue. She invited Jeannie and her younger brother, Johnny, over to a cookout after the ceremony, which was really a surprise graduation party for Jeannie. Even Ms. Rippetoe, her boss, came. Her dad was eager to come, too. And of course, Anna was there. One big happy family.

Marcus tapped a reply. "Will look at them on the desktop in a few. Anna couldn't make it. I'm home alone."

Marcus slipped into his running shorts and strolled into his kitchen and put on a kettle of water for some hot tea. Today a bowl of whole grain cereal with one-percent milk and a banana sounded just right. Marcus became a believer in eating right during his years of training for cross country. Marcus rarely ate solely for pleasure. Food was fuel.

His phone pinged again. Jeannie. "too bad. wish u were closer so u could come up and run the lake with me. think I can take u now. been training harder. mom and Nick back tomorrow. quiet has been nice. glad Lauren is just down the trail. she is amazing. makes me feel like family."

Marcus answered. "ur on next time up. Hitting Turkey Mtn trails this morning after breakfast. Send more pix."

Marcus hoped he could make the four-plus mile trail after the late night at Jazzy Jake's. True to form, Theresa was surrounded with friends she had made volunteering at a local food bank. *I'm impressed with how easily she connects and gets involved. I actually enjoyed being with her.*

Running stimulated him–therapy. It had a way of clearing his mind, listening to and feeling the slight changes in his body and breathing as he steadied into a rhythmic pace. Everything else fell away, and he needed the thought of Anna with Eric Greer to fall away before his imagination ran wild.

Jeannie chimed in again. "deal! ☺"

The teakettle whistled, and Marcus poured the boiling water over a bag of lemon ginger tea. He grabbed the cup and his breakfast and walked onto the balcony patio outside his living room. The morning was still cool and the giant oak in the center of the quadrangle shaded any sun that peaked over the southeastern corner of his unit. Another message alert interrupted the melody of his wind chimes. Anna this time. Marcus grabbed up the phone and read:

"Sorry about yesterday. Wish you could have seen the crowd. Eric was amazing. Had them in the palm of his hands. Media coverage fantastic. Donor brunch at 10:30. Running late. Will try to call tonight. Will tell you all about it."

And how was your day, Honey? Marcus thought as he laid the phone on the side table and took a sip of his tea. *If I don't have plans.* He swallowed a spoonful of cereal and picked up the phone and entered,

"What time?"

Anna replied a few seconds later, "10ish"

"ok. going to run around noon. Turkey Mtn."

"sounds fun. Want to hear about the cookout."

"later"

* * *

Marcus loved the runner's high. There was always that moment when he shifted into sort of an altered mental state when he wasn't consciously aware of the act of running. His form of meditation. Running came naturally. Cross country in high school and college, the paved park trails around Tulsa and Springfield, and now the more rugged trails through the countryside hills had become Marcus's sanctuary.

As much as he enjoyed Theresa's company, running was never going to be on her top ten list of ways to pass the afternoon. She was more the Zumba type. She said something about taking a spin class. Jeannie, on the other hand, gave him a run for his money around Community Lake. Fitness figured into her training as a dancer, as did yoga. Jeannie continually surprised him.

Today, Turkey Mountain's four mile yellow trail gave him the mental escape he needed. Running as much as possible, his thoughts drifted in and out of his time with Anna. *I was so certain of my feelings for her back in October. The first three months were blissful. Then, the Valentine weekend fiasco caught me by surprise. I thought Anna was ready to move to a more intimate relationship. Man, did I ever totally misread that. This whole Eric Greer campaign thing could really get in the way. Is Anna serious about us, or not? I'm not sure what the hell she's thinking. Or am I just making too much of this? Maybe we can sort it out tonight.*

By the time Marcus got back to the parking lot he felt purged. He had actually quit thinking about Anna and found his mind swirling around a recent tornado that had decimated Moore for a second time. Almost the same path as the '99 storm that had originally captured his attention as a youth. *There's got to be a better way to generate more efficiencies than our technology is getting us now. At some point I want to challenge my project team to start thinking about different ways of generating electricity from wind power. There's got to be a better way of getting the generation closer to the customer.*

Marcus's phone rang. He did not recognize the number—no one from his current contact list.

"Hello, this is Marcus."

A female voice replied, "Hi, Marcus. My name is Whitney Ellis. We haven't met, but I got your name this morning from a friend you met recently—Carmella Jenkins."

"Yes. Uh, yes, Carmella Jenkins. I met her briefly yesterday at a cookout. And her husband, uh," Marcus scanned his mind unsuccessfully for the name.

"Ron," Whitney added.

"Yeah, Ron. A real nice couple. Both doctors, right?"

"Right. They have a practice together. Anyway, Carmella thought we might have some things in common and suggested I give you a call. She got your number from a friend and said she thought it would be OK to call," Whitney explained with a twinge of hesitancy in her voice.

"Uh, yeah, I guess so." Marcus wasn't sure where this was headed.

"She said you are a supervisor at work and that you have some definite ideas about how someone our age could be an effective leader."

"Uh-huh. We talked about some of that yesterday."

"Well, let me get to the point. I'm in a group of young leaders that meets every couple of weeks. Kind of a social and professional networking group from different businesses in the area, and I want to invite you to join us."

"Humm. I've not heard of anything like that before. Sounds like it could be interesting."

"There's about twenty in the group right now from all kinds of businesses. We meet the first and third Thursday of the month after work for drinks and a brief presentation on leadership or management, something that helps us professionally. Sometimes we just hang out and talk. Sometimes we do lunch, and this Thursday we'll be meeting for lunch at Miguel's Taco Café. I wanted to invite you to meet up with us."

"Is everyone there a supervisor?" Marcus asked.

"Most, but not all. It's not a requirement. The group started with a few supervisors who were already friends, looking for a support group of like-minded people our age."

"Sure, OK. Just show up?"

"That's about it. May I text you a reminder?"

"Yeah. Fine. What do you do, Whitney?"

"Oh, I guess I should have mentioned that. I'm an account manager for a medical billing service. The Jenkins's practice is one of my accounts, and we got acquainted last year."

"Well, I look forward to meeting you Thursday. How will I recognize you?

"Oh, don't worry. I'll recognize you. Carmella shared the video of your leadership presentation with me. I watched it this morning. I was impressed with what you had to say. I'm sure I'll recognize you."

"That video seems to be getting around."

"You seemed very confident. And you make a great impression. You should think about doing more public speaking," Whitney said enthusiastically.

"Well, who knows what lies ahead? Right?"

"Right," Whitney concluded. "Then, I'll see you Thursday.

"It's on my calendar." Marcus concluded.

* * *

Marcus snapped to consciousness when the phone lying on his chest chirped and vibrated. *I must have dozed off . . . Anna . . . About time. What time is it? 11:15, damn. What happened to 10ish?*

Marcus put the phone to his ear without rising off the sofa where he had drifted off somewhere in the weather segment of the local 10 o'clock news. "Hello," he tried in vain to sound alert.

"Oh, I woke you," Anna began.

"I guess so, but that's OK. It's good to hear your voice

finally," Marcus was coming to.

"It's just been so hectic the last three days. I've been going non-stop. I started not to call since it's so late, but I promised," Anna sounded apologetic.

"I'm glad you did. I missed having you down here this weekend. It wasn't the weekend I had imagined."

"I know. Me neither. I was so looking forward to the cookout and being in Tulsa with you. I'm so sorry you had to go to the cookout alone."

"Well, I didn't exactly go alone."

Anna interrupted, her voice rising slightly, "Oh? You took a date?"

"Not exactly a date either," Marcus emphasized.

"Then exactly what?" Anna pressed.

"I invited Theresa Younger, you know, the person at work who's been introducing me around the oil and gas side of the company. I've told you about her."

"I remember, but why does she rate a date?"

"I didn't think of it that way. She's been a big help at work, introducing me around and all, and when you get a chance to go to a cookout at the home of your CEO's daughter, it's a big deal. I just thought it was a way to thank her for her kindness toward me. That's all." Anna was silent. Marcus continued, "Besides, you stood me up for a rich single guy running for congress."

Anna snapped back, "That's different. Eric is work. It's my job. That's not fair. The cookout was social. And when you take a girl with you to a social event, that's a date, if you ask me."

Marcus hesitated, surprised by Anna's reaction. Anna was quiet, her indignation obvious. *This is not the way I wanted this conversation to go. It's getting all twisted.* Marcus continued, "I'm sorry. I didn't mean to sound tacky. It was a reflex on my part to invite her out of courtesy and gratitude for her friendship. That's all."

Anna paused, then replied in a softer tone, "OK, then. If you say so."

"But I have to admit that I've been a little jealous of Greer because he's getting so much of your time. I feel like I'm getting squeezed out of your life. I don't get to see you everyday, and even our nightly phone calls have fallen off. I feel like you're slowly drifting away."

"I feel like I'm being pulled in so many directions, Marcus. My firm has committed me to Eric's campaign, but I still have a workload in addition that I cannot let slide. I was barely able to eek out time for Jeannie's graduation last week, as you know."

"I get it, Anna. It's just that you speak of Eric in such glowing terms and go on and on about him, and we aren't talking about where our relationship is headed. And," Marcus stopped.

"And what?" Anna prodded.

Marcus paused before continuing at a lower, slower tone and rate, "And here we are at June the first. The date you asked for back in February before we discussed a more exclusive and intimate relationship. It's like we just dropped the subject."

Anna matched Marcus's tone, "I know. I don't want to feel pressured into a relationship I'm not ready for yet. Going there would change everything between us, and I think that would be more than we can handle right now."

"I'm not sure I even understand what our relationship is," Marcus continued. "I knew the first time I laid eyes on you at Andy's soccer match that I wanted you in my life. I was willing to do whatever is necessary to spend as much time with you as possible. Lauren told me that first weekend that I was schmockered by you."

Anna giggled, "Schmockered? Is that even a word?"

"I know. That's what I asked Lauren when she said it." They laughed together, breaking the tension. "Anyway, whatever you call it, she was right."

"I guess the feeling was mutual. I couldn't wait to talk to my cousin, Erin, when I found out that you worked with her. I knew what Lauren was up to, and I was a willing participant," Anna reminisced.

"I didn't mean to put so much pressure on you to move into an intimate relationship so soon. I thought it was important that I tell you what I wanted," Marcus admitted.

"I get it. I just think rushing it isn't necessary." Anna paused. A deep sigh pushed through the phone before she continued. "That happened to me right after I started college. I drifted into a relationship that turned into an ugly possessive obsession. It nearly cost me my scholarship and my shot at college. I swore I would never move too quickly again, and I haven't," Anna confessed.

"You've never talked about that before," Marcus reflected.

"It's just that so much is happening so fast right now. I never in a thousand years would have thought I would get the chance to be involved in a political campaign of this importance so soon in my career. I'm learning so much from Greer's legal team. And I didn't realize I would get so interested in the political process. It's fascinating and exciting. I want to share that with you. That's why I think you might actually like Eric, and I want you to meet him," Anna's excitement crept back in.

"I guess I took all that excitement as you being attracted to him."

"Not in that way, Marcus. I'm sorry if I gave you the wrong impression about Eric." Anna said.

"And no need for you to feel jealous of Theresa. She knows I'm with you. She understands and respects the boundaries."

"Marcus, we're both going through so much change right now in our professional lives."

"Yeah, tell me about it," Marcus interjected.

Anna continued the thought, "So much change. I just think we should let things play out, and we'll know when it's time to move forward."

"But when will I see you again? This is not the kind of change I had in mind. How can we give a relationship a chance if we don't spend more time together?"

"Can you come to Springfield next weekend?"

"Wish I could. I head to Montana next Monday for the week. Got a lot to get done before I leave."

"Sounds like we're both swamped with work," Anna sighed. "So the trip with Jim Bob worked out?"

"Yeah, easier than I thought. Didn't even have to take annual leave after all."

I don't know why you're bothering with that little jerk.

"I decided if that situation is going to change I have to make the first move." Marcus explained.

"And why does that situation need to change? Remember what a jerk he was when he came up to as after the run and insulted you to your face?"

"Yeah, yeah, yeah," Marcus tried to soften Anna's sudden ire.

"Called you a pretty boy, or, or, or, a wind boy, just playing in the wind, or something like that," Anna persisted.

"Yeah, I remember."

"And how he squinted when he talked—like his eyes were synchronized to squint when his mouth moved?" Anna wouldn't let up.

"I know, I know, all that is still vivid in my mind. But like him or not, Jim Bob is well respected for his skill by the oil and gas side. If I'm going to be an example of leadership for the company, I've got to be willing to make those changes personally that others might not be willing to do," Marcus said.

Anna sighed, "I guess that's why I'm so attracted to you, Marcus. I know you're proud of your accomplishments, but you can see the bigger picture, too."

"I hope so. At least I think I'm beginning to," Marcus replied.

"Just hang in there with me, Marcus. Don't give up on us too quickly just because we aren't getting everything we want right now."

"A leader must be willing to make the changes personally that others are hesitant to do."

"OK. I guess I can do that," Marcus agreed.

Marcus and Anna ended the call and Marcus relocated to his bed. He couldn't remember the last time he had held Anna in a prolonged embrace. As he drifted into slumber it was the lingering feeling of Theresa's embrace the night before that comforted him.

3. No appetite for change

The aroma from Miguel's Taco Café infused the immediate vicinity of industrial buildings, announcing its presence before Marcus spotted the café tucked into the back of a jammed parking lot obscured by the '70s era warehouses. *I wonder why I haven't heard of this place? Am I that out of touch with the local food scene?* The banana yellow cinder block building decorated with bright orange and green geckos struck Marcus as cliché. *Damn. Fifteen minutes late. Whitney probably thinks I stood her up.*

Marcus stepped into the tiny foyer of the crammed café. Miguel's obviously was not the first restaurant to occupy this space. The furnishings were leftovers from the variety of eateries that had preceded it. The happy rhythm of Mexican music blared over the conversations happening above mounds of chips and salsa and plates heaped with generous portions of entrees.

Rosa, the hostess approached, "¡Hola. Welcome to Miguel's. Are you Mister Marcus?" she happily inquired.

"Yes. Yes I am," Marcus replied, pleasantly surprised.

"Miss Whitney asked I watch for you. She show me your picture. This way, please." Rosa zig zagged Marcus though the narrow openings between chair backs, to a private dining room. "Enjoy, Mister Marcus," she held the door for him as he squeezed by.

A woman, deep in conversation with two men at her table, sat facing the entry to the room. She glanced up as

Marcus started toward her. Obviously recognizing him, she interrupted her conversation, waving and standing up in the aisle in a single motion. Her toothy white smile radiated from a caramel complexion. A mane of tight curly black hair framed her round face. She offered her hand as Marcus approached.

"Marcus, so glad you made it. I'm Whitney Ellis. I saved you a place."

"Sorry I'm late. I got delayed at work, and then there was construction–"

"Not a problem," Whitney interrupted, "Just thrilled you could make it. Please," Whitney motioned to the empty chair, speaking to the two men as she slipped back into her seat, "This is Marcus Winn from Millennium Energy, my guest. Marcus this is Thomas Spires with HydroTek and Ramin Tehrani with Memorial Medical Center."

"My pleasure," Marcus said, offering handshakes. " Please, go ahead with your lunch."

Whitney began by catching Marcus up on the discussion, "Marcus, we were just talking about some of the changes our companies are going through. Right now in my billing company we are ramping up to convert to new medical billing system required by the insurance industry. It not only affects our staff, but also the office managers of our clients. It's a mess."

"The important thing is that we are willing to make those changes," Marcus offered, trying to sound positive.

"I know, but once people get used to doing things a certain way, they don't like being forced to change, especially when they think their way is good enough," Ramin countered. "In the health care industry I don't feel as if I have too much control one way or another," Ramin went on. "A big hospital chain recently bought Memorial, and now I'm struggling to learn their way of doing things. No one asks me what I think. They just tell me what to do."

"At HydroTek we build water well drilling rigs and ship them all over the world," Thomas said. "Lately, we've been affected by the conflicts in the Middle East where we ship a lot of a our rigs."

"Sounds like we all get bumped around by change," Marcus replied.

Thomas continued, "Yeah, there's the international side, then there's the problem with finding and keeping good welders. The pipelines hire them away with big wages, about twice what we can pay."

Marcus added, "My business, renewable energy, is itself a disruptive industry, and most people don't really get it. Sometimes the reason behind the change we are pushing for is not obvious. All they see is their narrow view of how they think the change will make life either better or worse for them individually. The bigger picture is not important to them."

"I know. Why change if you don't see what's in it for you. Right?" Thomas added.

"That's what I hear all the time from some of our staff. All they see about the new billing system is how much more work it will be for them to learn and implement," Whitney agreed.

Ramin interjected, before completely finishing a bite of taco, "So, how do we get our staff past their resistance?"

A waiter came to the table, "What for you, señor?" looking at Marcus.

"How about a couple of pork tacos?"

"Small order, tres, OK?" the waiter explained holding up three fingers.

"OK, yes."

"Sí. To drink?"

"Just water, please."

"Sí, ¡gracias!" and the waiter squeezed between the chairs toward the kitchen.

"This place is the best," Ramin continued.

"My first time here," Marcus admitted.

"Well, I predict it won't be your last," Ramin affirmed. "The food here is nothing like you get at a chain restaurant. I don't get it. How can Americans take fresh ingredients and turn them into junk food?"

"I'm paying more attention to my diet since I've started training again," Marcus said.

"You look in pretty good shape," Thomas said.

"I was starting to lose it. Then I met my girlfriend in October, and she inspired me to get back into a routine of running and light weight training."

"Yuck. The thought of going to a gym every day. Not gonna happen," Thomas confessed.

"I think most people try to do too much too quickly and end up getting burned out or injured," Marcus said. "Slow and easy is the best way to make the changes over the long haul, and make them last."

"Well, there's no time for easy-does-it at my company. We're always in a rush to get billings out." Whitney said. Thomas and Ramin nodded their agreement.

"Back to the resistance issue," Marcus redirected the conversation, "maybe people just feel more comfortable with what they know, and they push back because they feel like they're being set up to fail. How far in advance are they getting trained up for it?"

"The workday is hectic enough without taking staff off task. We have a series of tutorials on line that associates can watch when they need a question answered.

"Most people try to do too much too quickly and end up getting burned out. . . Slow and easy is the best way to make the changes over the long haul, and make them last."

Our vendor claims that will be enough. They call it 'just in time training,'" Whitney explained.

"I'm just saying that if you listen to the staff's exact words, they are probably telling you why they are resisting. You know, what it is that's stressing them," Marcus offered. "I know from my own experience that I start to feel the stress when I'm not getting what I need, want, or expect."

The waiter returned with Marcus's order and placed the plate with three warm corn tacos in front of him. "Everything OK? More sauce?"

"Looks fine. I think we're OK for now," Marcus replied

No sooner had Marcus received his meal than Whitey stood up at her place to address the room, "Hey, everyone," she raised her hand above her head and gave it a quick wave. "Hey, everyone," she repeated, and the room hushed. "Welcome to our lunch meet up. I see a couple of new faces, and I want to introduce my guest. This is

Marcus Winn from Millennium Energy. He leads a wind-field project team. With his permission, I'll send out his contact information." Marcus nodded his agreement.

Whitney stepped through her usual routine to introduce guests and make announcements. Then, she asked, "How many of you are sitting with at least one person you are meeting for the first time?" She raised her hand, and about half the room did likewise. "Good then. One of our objectives is to meet new people, and it looks like we are doing a fairly good job at it. Remember, we do have some other meet ups planned at different places. Our goal is to help you connect with other supervisors so we can support each other and learn from each other's experiences. I know we've only been doing this for a few months. I think we need a Facebook page for the group–"

At the word, "Facebook," a hand shot up from a tall blonde standing in the back of the room waiving enthusiastically, "I'll do it, Whitney. I'll set one up. Just tell me what to call it."

"Ok, then, Abby," Whitney grinned widely, "I guess that's settled. Get with me after we wrap up."

About 12:50 the room began thinning. Several others came up to Marcus and introduced themselves. Whitney signaled Marcus to wait up. "Marcus, would it be OK if I just called you occasionally to talk about some common supervisor issues? You know, talk shop a little?"

"Sure. Yeah. That would be fine. I'm sure that would be mutually helpful," Marcus agreed.

Marcus headed back to the JEE campus. He had some planning to do for his trip to Montana on Monday.

4. Boomtown

If destiny is the sum total of choices that bring one to a particular moment, Marcus wondered what were the sequence of choices that put him onboard a Johnstone Energy corporate jet at 6:30 a.m. on a June Monday morning, 39,000 feet somewhere above the Great Plains on his way to Williston, North Dakota, sitting across the aisle from a foul-mouth drilling engineer he had agreed to spend the next four days with touring drilling sites in the Bakken shale play?

"Having second thoughts?" Jim Bob Danner's scratchy high-pitched voice broke through the jet engine's whine leaking into the cabin.

"Not in the least. Been looking forward to it," Marcus said, turning to acknowledge Jim Bob's comment.

Jim Bob spat a sliver of a fingernail he had just chewed from his left pinky into his palm. He nervously bounced his right knee up and down. Earlier in the hanger Jim Bob had made it glaringly clear that Marcus was not welcome on the flight. "How the hell did you get on this hop, Wind Boy," Jim Bob scowled when Marcus appeared. "Thought you would catch a commercial flight. This hop ain't for no damned sightseers." Jim Bob stepped in front of Marcus, impeding his path to the aircraft.

"Just reporting as directed," Marcus hesitated for a split second before walking around Jim Bob and up the plane's airstair.

Like he told Anna last week, Marcus felt he needed

to lead by example, so he reached out to Jim Bob and offered to understand Jim Bob's world rather than demanding that Jim Bob respect his first.

Marcus's travel arrangements came down from the C-suite. He had not given being on the flight a second thought. He had been looking forward to his first trip on a corporate jet. Still the idea of spending the week with a man who had introduced himself two months ago by insulting him made Marcus queasy.

Jim Bob had a point, though. Marcus was an unlikely passenger. All sixteen seats were taken with managers and technicians who deployed from the Tulsa headquarters of Johnstone Oil and Gas at least twice a month to check on production, new drilling, and other matters. Several had opened laptops. Others sat with eyes closed. Just a routine commute for everyone, except him.

"Got lucky that so many needed to go up this week. Usually, we're on the King Air. It's smaller and slower. Wonder who you bumped for that seat?"

Marcus decided not to take Jim Bob's bait for an argument, "How often do you come up?"

"Every three or four weeks," Jim Bob answered. "Better be glad you picked June to tag along. Winters are brutal. No country for softies."

Marcus ignored the dig. "How long have you been doing this?" Marcus asked.

"Drillin' or working for Johnstone?"

"Both, I guess," Marcus replied, not realizing his question had been ambiguous. "I mean, how long have you been a drilling engineer?"

"Been with Johnstone for three years. Been on drilling rigs ever since my daddy would let me tag along. Stepped onto my first one near Midland when we lived out there.

Got an ass whuppin' for doing it, too," Jim Bob chuckled as he rubbed his calloused hands together, as if an ass whuppin' was a badge of honor.

Jim Bob obviously wanted to tell his story. Marcus smiled and chuckled, too, but said nothing.

"I was ten. Dad let me ride to a site one Saturday morning to check on a problem. He told me to stay put in the truck, but I got curious and ran up onto the plat-form where it looked like the action was. Dad grabbed me up and stuffed me back into the truck, but not before thrashing my ass good. Told me it was to let me know how dangerous it was out there. But I was hooked. I was amazed at the size of everything—the rig, the tools, the noise, the men. I wanted to be part of it. My dad was bigger than life to me."

"You obviously admire him."

"Admire, yeah," Jim Bob paused and glanced a moment out his window and before turning toward Marcus. "He was like a god to me. Massive. All I ever wanted was to be like him, only better."

"Elliot Sloan tells me you are. That's why I wanted to tag along."

"Well, I'm not sure what to think about you yet, wind boy" Jim Bob squinted as he spoke. "You must have some stroke. The only reason I offered to let you tag along is I didn't think there was an ice cube's chance in hell anyone would agree to it. They don't let people just tag along . . . especially if they ain't oil. So I guess they'll be watching that I show you a good time, or at least get you back in one piece." Jim Bob sounded resigned to his duties with Marcus.

Marcus paused to measure his words, also realizing that the other passengers were not tuned into their conversation. "All the same, I want to see ground level how your side of the business works. Fair enough?"

"Be prepared for the full Monty. I can't wait around for stragglers."

"I expected nothing less," Marcus smiled and turned his gaze back to the view from over seven miles above the earth.

Marcus was amazed at the number of well sites dotting the landscape he could see as the jet descended on its landing approach. Most of what he saw was collection sites where wells had been completed. "How many rigs do you have running right now?" Marcus asked.

"Got ten drilling and four getting setup," Jim Bob answered.

"How many will we see?"

"About half of 'em if everything goes according to plan," Jim Bob beamed.

Marcus could see a shuttle with a Johnstone Enterprises logo waiting for them outside the JEE hanger when they taxied to a stop. There was no flight attendant to tell everyone to stay seated with their seat belt on. But no one rushed to get off. Everyone knew the routine. "The ground crew will take care of the luggage," Jim Bob explained. "We're going to the field office to get our truck, and we're heading out. No time to waste."

"Sounds like a plan," Marcus agreed.

"Rigs run 24-7, so schedule ain't a problem. And this time of year, hell, the sun don't even set until around ten," Jim Bob sounded gleeful at the prospects.

"You're in your world here, aren't you?" Marcus noticed Jim Bob's energy pick up.

"Damn straight, wind boy. Damn straight."

The ride from the airport down state highway 2 revealed a Williston that had mushroomed into a boom-town in western North Dakota. The population had been stable at around 14,000 for a decade, but now was well on its way to doubling in a couple of years, according to projections. The change was both good and bad. The local economy was booming. Real estate values skyrocketed. Hotel chains couldn't build fast enough, from the more posh corporate oriented to the low-end no frills bargain brands. Marcus wondered what would happen when the boom went bust, as they usually do. For now, though, it looked like things in Williston were prospering.

The shuttle arrived at the Johnstone complex on the southwest edge of town just off the highway. A metal building with a stone façade and the JEE logo on the front was easily visible from the road. The van dropped every-one off at the front door and disappeared before everyone could get inside. Some of the Johnstone staff headed back into the office complex, thinning out the group by half. A young woman approached Jim Bob and the other arrivals with keys, which she handed over when signed for. She noticed the new face.

"Hey, Jim Bob, got your usual truck," she batted her eye lashes and smiled as she laid the keys in Jim Bob's open hand, letting her fingers brush his palm lightly.

"Thanks, Patti. I appreciate the way you look out for me," he smiled back speaking in the softest tone Marcus had yet heard come from him.

"Did you bring a friend?" she asked, looking Marcus over.

"Not really. Just a guy from one of Johnstone's other companies who wanted to find out what it's like in the oil patch," Jim Bob's usual tone returned without bothering to introduce Marcus.

"Well, he's mighty pretty." Patti looked Marcus over head to toe. "I bet Desiree would like to meet him if you boys are up for a drink tonight."

"Better take a rain check on that, Patti," Jim Bob rattled the keys on the key ring. "I've gotta give wind boy, here a rig education, and it's going to be late nights and early mornings this week."

"Wind boy? What kind of a name is that?" Patti embraced the clipboard to her chest.

Marcus finally spoke, "Hi Patti. My name is Marcus. I'm an engineer with Millennium Energy. I run a windfarm in western Oklahoma."

"Windfarm? Why we've got a big one of those right north of here."

"I noticed it as we landed," Marcus said smiling.

"My, my, boys. Oil and wind running around together. Kinda like dogs and cats living together. This ought to be interesting. Sure you boys don't want to get together tonight? Like I said, Desiree would get a kick out of you," she offered again aiming a big smile at Marcus.

"Maybe later, Patti," Jim Bob cut in. "Right now we gotta hit the road. I'll catch up with you later, OK?"

"OK, if you say so, Jim Bob," Patti batted her eyes again at Jim Bob, then turned to Marcus, "Hey, wind boy, Jim Bob is the best driller there is. He'll teach you a thing or two."

"I'm sure he will," Marcus said as he turned to follow Jim Bob toward the back door leading to the motor pool.

"And a hell of a two-stepper," Patti shouted at them leaving.

Jim Bob stopped cold and spun around, "Damn it, Patti, you're killing my image here." Jim Bob spun back around and headed out the door. "Jeez," he exclaimed shaking his head.

Marcus couldn't resist grinning, "Don't worry, Jim Bob. Your secret is safe with me."

"Shut up, damn it," Jim Bob stepped up his pace, "and keep up."

This might be different than I thought, Marcus matched Jim Bob's gait.

"And don't ask me any stupid questions, wind boy," Jim Bob hopped into the cab and slammed the door.

* * *

Jim Bob had nothing to say as he aimed the white three-quarter-ton pickup west. Marcus had no idea where they were headed or how far out in the boonies they were going. One thing for sure, after about an hour of silence, Jim Bob clearly was not much for casual conversation. Talk would have been drowned out anyway by the blaring country music Jim Bob had dialed in shortly after passing Williston's city limits.

"Got a favorite country singer?" Marcus took a stab at breaching the conversational wall.

"What's it to ya?" Jim Bob barely glanced sideways.

"I like Garth Brooks and Blake Shelton. Oklahoma boys you know," Marcus offered.

"Figures," Jim Bob shook his head once, feigning disgust and rolling his eyes, as if Marcus got his favorites wrong.

"Why do you say that? Figures. What's wrong with 'em?"

"Pretty boys. Brooks is just a Vegas entertainer now, and Shelton is a wannabe. Neither of 'em a workin' man."

"So what's your idea of country singer?" Marcus turned slightly to the left, adjusting his seat belt.

"Trace Adkins," Jim Bob said emphatically. "Now there's a man who knows life and loss. Worked on an oil rig. Had his nose torn half off in a car wreck. Got his left pinky cut off and had the doctors sew it back on, crooked on purpose, so he could play his guitar. Even got shot in the heart and lived to tell about it. Not afraid to speak his mind neither. Yep, Trace is my kind of guy. And a Louisiana boy, like me."

"I can see why you would like him," Marcus let Jim Bob have this round. At least they were talking.

A few minutes passed, then Jim Bob said, "Didn't take you for a country fan."

"I'm not totally depraved. After all, I went to college at Oklahoma State, and you can't call yourself a cowboy without learning to two-step and do the Cotton-eyed Joe and hollar, 'bullshit,' out of the blue every once in a while. And Garth Brooks graduated there, so I guess that's another reason I like him. Just got his MBA, you know. Class of 2011. Walked down the aisle with his classmates. No honorary degree, no limelight. Just an average guy. That's what I like about him."

"I took you for the soft jazz type. You know, a glass of red wine and some Kenny G."

"You know Kenny G?" Marcus asked, surprised.

"Not really, but I ain't totally deprave either. My dad loved jazz of all types, and being from half-way between New Orleans and Memphis, I got a jazz education growing up around him."

Jim Bob turned down a dirt road kicking up the dust behind the truck. "Almost there, Wind Boy."

"So, what should I do when we get there? What do I need to know?" Marcus felt his heart rate pick up in anticipation.

""Stand where I tell you and don't ask any questions. Just watch and listen. I'm here to work, not educate or entertain you. And keep you damn hardhat on. Don't take it off unless I take mine off. What do you know about the oil patch?"

"Not really anything. That's why I wanted to see first hand."

"Damnit. This is gonna be a long four days." Jim Bob turned into a well site. "This rig is just about ready to start drilling. I need to make sure everything is set up to my specifications. The toolpusher is pretty much on the ball, but the driller and I don't always see eye-to-eye." Jim Bob stopped the truck and got out. Marcus met him at the front of the truck. "Here, Wind Boy," Jim Bob handed Marcus his notebook. "Keep up with this in case I need it. And get that shit-eatin' grin off your face. It's time to go to work."

For the next four hours Marcus watched Jim Bob in action. He went over every detail of the operation, none of it Marcus understood. It was an entirely foreign language, and the technology was a complete mystery. What he did understand was that most of the set up was spot on. The crew had a few questions of clarification for Jim Bob, which he answered. Only once did he seem putout at the driller, Mickey, over some issue that Jim Bob thought was abundantly clear in his instructions, but Mickey had gotten wrong.

Marcus and Jim Bob went back to the truck. "It's about thirty minutes to the next rig." Jim Bob reached behind Marcus's seat and flipped open an ice chest. "Here, Wind Boy. Don't want you passing out on me." Jim Bob tossed Marcus a sandwich. "Ham and cheese. Patti packs me a lunch on the first day. Always over does it. It's gotta last 'till about nine tonight."

"Thanks. I never thought about bringing lunch with me today," Marcus started unwrapping the sandwich. "Any water—," Jim Bob produced a bottled water before Marcus could get the rest of the question out, and closed the lid on ice chest.

"Tomorrow you're on your own," Jim Bob said as he started the engine.

"I have a new appreciation for the technical complexity of a rig," Marcus said after swallowing his first bite of the sandwich.

"So what the hell did you think we did? Just punch a hole in the ground, and presto, oil flows out?"

"I knew there was more to it than that. I just didn't realize how much more. Seeing things up close is impressive," Marcus took a swig of water.

"Well you ain't seen nothin' yet. The next rig is drilling, but it ain't making the progress I expected. No amount of discussing it on the phone has helped, and I predict there will be some serious butt-chewing."

"Well, I'll make sure I stay out of the way," Marcus finished his sandwich and went quiet. Marcus knew when he got back to the room tonight he would be searching for how oil rigs worked just so he might have some idea of the terminology and jargon.

Jim Bob gulped the last of his water and wiped his mouth with his sleeve. "How do you do it, Wind Boy? How do you pull it off?"

Jim Bob's question came out of left field. "What do you mean? How do I pull what off?" Marcus crumpled the just emptied plastic bottle, puzzled where Jim Bob was going. But he didn't have to wait long to find out.

"Keep two women happy. Theresa from work and that

hot Mexican girl you had at the run. How do you get to have two hot women and now Patti wants to introduce you to her best friend in the whole damn world?"

Flabbergasted, "First of all, Jim Bob, my personal life is none of your business. And second I don't have anything at all going with Theresa. We're just friends."

"Bul-l-l-l-l shit, Wind Boy," Jim Bob spat out, "You expect me to believe you don't have special benefits with both those hotties? Look at you. Athletic, citified, sharp dresser, a goddamn You Tube celebrity, big man on campus. I mean, I see you and Theresa in the cafeteria. She's all ga-ga over you, man. And I saw that señorita loving on you. And you expect me to think you ain't in the middle of that? I repeat, bul-l-l-l-l shit."

"Man, Jim Bob, you are just crude. But, OK, it's just you and me here in this truck, and if what you want is to go mano-a-mano with me, then give me your best fuckin' shot, cause I'm not going to put up with your endless bullshit for the next four days. What's your goddamn problem? I'm on your turf here, so let's get it on."

Jim Bob hit the brakes. The truck skidded to a stop on the gravel access road built between drilling sites. Jim Bob slammed the gearshift into park, but left the truck running. "All right, Wind Boy, no holds barred." Jim Bob released his seat belt and turned as far as he could to face Marcus. "All my life I've had to take it from pretty boys like you who get what they want without doing the work. Whether it's the good jobs, the best grades, or the hot girls, everything comes easy 'cause you have an ass kissing way of getting by—all your sweet talkin', politically correct, silver-tongued drivel. Makes me wanna puke.

"While guys like me bust our ass to scrape out our due. Nothin' comes easy. I guarantee you that if I weren't the son of Archie Danner I wouldn't have this job. Look at me, man. Can you honestly say I have a chance with any girl like Theresa. If there was a picture in the dictionary beside the word 'redneck,' it would be mine. I'm under no illusion about my looks.

"Archie Danner, on the other hand, was a big man with thick dark hair. I always wondered why I didn't take after him. Everyone said I favored my mother's side. When I got older I figured out the math on my own and realized I couldn't be Archie's natural son. But I had the good fortune of being loved and raised by him as his own, and all I've wanted to do is to honor him. But even that was taken away from me when he was killed in a rig accident because some kiss-ass pretty boy oil executive skimped on safety for a few extra dollars profit.

"I worked the shit jobs to learn the rigs from the ground up. Book smarts come hard for me. But I wanted to be an engineer, so I slogged my way through college. Didn't party or chase girls. Got through the math and chemistry by sheer force of will, and when the first job offers came in after college, they were the left-overs. But I took 'em, and I worked 'em, and I took all kinds of shit from pretty boy engineers who had book smarts but no rig smarts, and who were just too fuckin' lazy to do the work. And I worked rings around 'em.

"My numbers spoke for me. Aaron Jackson noticed my work, and called me. Then he found out I was Archie's boy, and he offered me a chance. And I performed. I've delivered for Johnstone. But, damnit, I won't stand for sloppy work or for people who don't do their homework. That's why there's goin' to be some ass chewing at the next rig. I don't get to hire and fire or run a rig, but I won't let half-ass slide, and I'm not afraid to call it like I see it. Popularity is not my purpose in life. I might be a bastard child and a son-of-a-bitch to some, but when I lay my head down at night, I sleep with a clear conscience, because I will not be out worked by anyone.

"So, I see you get on that jet this morning, knowing at least five guys who deserved to be on it in front of you, but had to take an extra day up and back on commercial flights to get here for the week. And all I know about you is you made a couple of fancy speeches, I haven't seen anything that tells me you earned your way on that plane. Whatever pretty boy strokes you got with the higher ups don't impress me one bit." Jim Bob's face glowed a fiery red, and he leaned in toward Marcus. Spittle leaked out the corner of his mouth and dribbled toward his chin. Jim Bob wiped it off with the back of his hand. He wasn't done.

"Educating you is not my fuckin' job this week, Wind Boy. But here you are. So you have an opportunity to get up close and personal with a drilling rig. Show me you are worth my goddamn time, and maybe we have something to talk about." Jim Bob held his glare as he went silent and leaned back toward the door. Nothing but the sound of the engine idling and the truck's air conditioner compressor kicking on intruded into the cab.

Marcus sat quietly, contemplating his response. *Deflect and redirect. Deflect and redirect. Give yourself time to think about what Jim Bob said. Don't just react to the verbal attack. Jim Bob's rant was more about himself than about me. Don't even go there over Theresa and Anna. That's not the issue here. Jim Bob was just baiting me, goading me. Deal with the core of what Jim Bob was saying. Deal with his perception that I, and people like me, have it easy. I've got to change Jim Bob's perception of me. I also must respond to Jim Bob's self-esteem.*

Marcus began calmly, "You've given me a lot to think about, Jim Bob. First of all, I'm sorry you lost your dad that way. I hadn't heard that part of the story. He sounds like a man I also would have admired. Second, you're right. Some people do schmooze by on something other than their ability, and I agree it isn't fair or right. I had no idea that a seat on the corporate jet carried such symbolic importance.

"All I can say is that I can think of a dozen places I rather be than Nowhere, Montana, and a hundred people I'd rather be with right now. But I'm here to learn and see for myself, because I want to earn the respect of Nelson Johnstone and others in oil and gas. And Elliot Sloan, who you know, my mentor, and a man I admire and trust, says you're one of the best at what you do.

"I have no control over my looks, except my grooming and physical fitness, or yours for that matter. What you think about yourself is up to you, but I've already met one person today who apparently sees something in you—that Patti obviously has a thing for you, and she's a pretty attractive girl, in my opinion. So you must have some redeeming quality as a human being.

"Go ahead, call me Wind Boy all you want. I don't give a shit. Neither do I care what you think about my relationship with Theresa and Anna, or any other woman for that matter. My conscience is clear.

"Neither do I care what you think about renewable energy —wind energy in particular. I'm in it because I love it the same way you love the oil patch. I do know one day all the oil will be sucked out of the ground, but the wind will still be blowing. In the meantime, we're all in this together, and we get to decide how we are going to act toward each other. So, call me a pretty boy all you want, I can't stop you. But I'll do my best to earn my way and to be a decent human being at the same time, so when I lie down at night I can sleep with a clear conscience." Marcus finished, looking Jim Bob squarely in his narrow eyes.

Jim Bob cleared his throat, squared up behind the stirring wheel without saying a word, put the truck in gear and kicked up gravel as he gunned it toward the next drilling site.

Back at the hotel that night Marcus went on line to bone up on drilling technology. He brought his notes along on the ride. Every day made more sense to him. Jim Bob was less hostile on Tuesday. As promised, Jim Bob set a fast pace. He began explaining some of what happened as he and Marcus traveled between well sites, but there was no more personal chit-chat. Thursday arrived before Marcus could look up. True to his word, Jim Bob had worked hard and set a grueling pace. Now, it was time to relax.

* * *

Jim Bob sat across the booth from Marcus at Outfitters, one of the local bars that had sprung up in Williston during the boom. It attracted mostly the transient workers who had poured in from all over to claim the high wage and physically demanding oil patch jobs. The locals kept to themselves in their established hangouts. Jim Bob accounted for three of the six empty beer bottles on the table. The other three belonged to Marcus, Patti, who sat snuggled up to Jim Bob, and Desiree, who wanted to snuggle up to Marcus despite his efforts to keep an appropriate distance. This was the last night of the trip, and

Marcus was eager to catch the flight back to Tulsa the
next afternoon. He had not spoken to Anna since leaving
Tulsa, neither had she texted. Theresa texted her, "bon
voyage," Monday; otherwise, he had been incommunicado
while hitting two, and sometimes, three rigs a day with
Jim Bob.

Marcus had decided there were two Jim Bobs. One
was the cocky, and often demeaning, know-it-all who did
not hesitate to strip any rig hand bare of all dignity when
he was displeased with their performance. Marcus was
certain that Jim Bob's castigating diatribes, like he witnessed Monday afternoon and again Wednesday, would
make even Gunnery Sergeant Hartman in the movie *Full
Metal Jacket* weep. Then, there was the Jim Bob across
from him now, sitting up close to Patti like he was stuffed
with a soft marshmallow filling. Which was the real Jim
Bob? Marcus thought he knew.

While out on the rigs and in the truck traveling between well sites, Jim Bob kept that hard edge. That was
the tough, self-assured persona Jim Bob projected. Why?
Marcus did not know. And he wondered why Jim Bob
even let him see this kinder, gentler side of him. Patti
and Desiree met Jim Bob and Marcus at Outfitters, and
Marcus was not sure whether that was by happenstance
or if Patti and Jim Bob had arranged it so that it looked
coincidental for Marcus's sake. Regardless, there they
were, and here he was, trying to be kind and cordial to
Desiree while keeping a gentlemanly distance.

"Come on, Marcus. Relax. That girlfriend down in
Missouri you've been talking about won't never find out
if you have a dance or two with me." Then Desiree stared
into Jim Bob's eyes and confirmed rhetorically, "Will she,
Jim Bob?"

"Not a peep from me," Jim Bob agreed with a wave of his beer bottle, then took the last sip and signaled the server for another round.

"What's the matter, Marcus, ain't I your type?" Desiree teased looping her right arm through the bend of Marcus's left arm. "I'm not a lawyer like your girlfriend, but I am somewhat educated, you know. I have a degree. I'm an R-N. And I am a charge nurse in maternity at the Medical Center. I'm probably never gonna see you again after tonight, and you're gonna deny me just one dance?" Almost on cue, the house band broke into a ballad, "Come on, Marcus, here's a slow one. All you gotta do is hold me and sway side to side," Desiree stood up from her outside seat in the booth, taking Marcus's hand and tugging him gently.

"All right, I guess one dance would be OK." Marcus scooted out and Desiree led him to the dance floor as the lights dimmed.

Desiree put her left arm around Marcus's neck and pulled her tall slender frame tight against him. She was firm and toned. Desiree placed her forehead softly against Marcus's left cheek. He could feel her breath on his neck. He could feel his knees trying to lock.

"Relax, Wind Boy," Desiree whispered, "let all that locked up energy go. Just relax your shoulders and let your arms hold me while we move to the music. Give yourself to the music. You move and I'll move with you."

Marcus closed his eyes and let the music overwhelm him. *Anna and I never danced like this. I've never even held her this close. Even when we hug, it's not like she is giving herself to me like Desiree is making me feel right now. I didn't know it could feel so natural to hold a woman this way. And I don't even know her. All I know about*

Desiree is what she's told me and that she has a sweet personality . . . and that she's persistent. Am I wrong to like it?

"That's more like it," Desiree whispered lifting her head slightly, then returned her forehead to Marcus's cheek. This time she tightened her hold around his neck slightly, and Marcus pulled her closer so that he could feel his body against hers all the way to his knees. The band reached the final bars of the ballad, "Don't let go," Desiree looked up to Marcus. "Stay, they usually play two or three slow ones in a row." She firmed her embrace. Marcus complied.

Soon, Marcus found himself in that space during the dance when it felt like he and Desiree were the only couple on the floor and the song was written just for them. *Am I being bewitched or something? Why does it feel like I'm holding someone who's intimately familiar, but we've just met? Why do I hope there's a third song?* Marcus suddenly felt self-conscious at the first stirrings of arousal. *This is embarrassing.*

"Ummmmmmm," Desiree moaned without lifting her head and pressed seductively against Marcus raising her hips to match him, "that's more like it," and she kissed Marcus lightly on the neck.

Marcus's mind raced somewhere between pleasure and panic. *Why do I want her, but I know it's soooo wrong? Why do I want to stay in her arms all night and run for the door at the same time? Why do I want to linger in the fragrance of her hair, and force myself to see Anna's face to remind me of who I am?* Marcus realized the band had segued into a third ballad and he was holding Desiree even closer and that somewhere during the dance Desiree had placed her right hand on his chest and he had fully embraced her with his left, and he liked it.

"I can come to your room later, and no one will ever know," Desiree offered in a warm, breathy whisper.

The urges in Marcus were on fire. He tried to form the words, "I shouldn't," but they stuck somewhere short of the vocal cords, and all he could get out was the sound of clearing his throat.

"I'll take that as a maybe," Desiree said and kissed Marcus again on his neck.

A sharp jab on Marcus's left shoulder blade broke Desiree's spell, "I'm cutting in, fella." The final cords of the last ballad faded into the first beats of a swing, and the lights came back up to their usual dance floor level.

"Shit, Glen, what the hell are you doin'?" Desiree screamed at the intruder as she stepped around Marcus and pushed at Glen causing him to catch his balance on his heels.

"I'm just claimin' what's mine. That's all." Glen scowled at Marcus while looking past Desiree.

Desiree pushed at Glen again, "Don't you get it, Glen? Goddammit, I ain't yours, I never was yours, and I ain't never gonna be yours. That's what the restraining order is for, you asshole."

Marcus stepped toward Glen, "Come on, fella, leave the lady alone–"

"Lady? Is that what you think?" Glen obviously had had several drinks too many and wreaked of stale smoke, "she's just a dance floor tease and a two-bit whore."

"Then why all the bother?" Marcus took a stronger position between Glen and Desiree.

"Why, pretty boy, you hopin' to get some of that sweet stuff later tonight?"

"OK, that's enough. You had your say and it's time

to back off," Marcus tried to redirect Glen, staring him down, and extending his right arm slightly to protect Desiree.

"Why you–" and with that Glen let loose a wild roundhouse swing at Marcus, but Marcus saw it coming from the left out the corner of his eye and leaned back slightly to dodge the punch. The swing missed Marcus's chin and glanced off his right shoulder, but the follow through caught Desiree just below her left eye. Desiree, shrieked, grabbed her face and turned her back to Glenn as a reflex, as if she had used that defensive move before.

Instead of protecting himself, Marcus instinctively moved to grasp Desiree and shielding her from Glen. Marcus turned to see what Glen would do next.

Glen caught his balance and stood to mount another charge. A massive object torpedoed Glenn sending him flying across the dance floor and into a nearby table. Jim Bob regained his balance and pounced on Glen punching him once squarely on the left cheek. Then he flipped Glen onto his belly with one hand. Jim Bob put his knee in Glen's back and pinned his head on the floor with his massive hand. Glen was done just that quickly.

Jim Bob leaned down to Glen's ear, but spoke so everyone could hear, "OK, you pathetic piece of shit, I'm gonna stand you up now and you're gonna sincerely apologize to the lady and to my friend for your unseemly behavior. And then you are gonna leave quietly and you're never, and I mean NEVER, gonna come back in here again," Jim Bob raised up to look at the bartender, "ain't that right, Oscar?"

"Right, Jim Bob," Oscar replied.

Jim Bob continued, "And you are gonna leave the lady alone, and by alone I mean you're gonna mind every detail of that restraining order and make yourself into a goddamn model citizen. Am I right?"

"Right," Glen offered with a strained grunt, trying to catch his breath.

Jim Bob jerked Glen up to a full standing position with a single move. "To hell with an apology. How much money you got on you?" Jim Bob had Glenn by the back of his neck in a vice grip and shook him once

"Fifty. Maybe."

"Get it out and put it on the bar."

Glen reached into his left front pocket and pulled out a wad of bills and dropped them onto the bar.

"How much is that, Oscar?" Jim Bob kept both his grip and his eyes firmly locked on Glen.

"I count forty-seven."

"Will that cover my tab?"

"Yep, with some left for a tip."

With that Jim Bob turned Glen toward the door and spoke again into his ear so everyone could hear, "Now you go home into the quiet corner of your room and you reflect on what just happened here. And you get down on your knees and you thank Jesus that you got out of here tonight without any severe injuries. And you reflect on the shitty ways you've treated Desiree over the years and become convicted in your soul that you will repent of that before it costs you more than forty-seven dollars. Are you a believer, asshole? Are you a believer?" Jim Bob shook Glenn twice, causing him to lose his balance slightly, then stabilized him with his grip.

"I'm a believer," Glen choked out a weepy reply.

"Louder, sinner!" Jim Bob screamed in his ear.

"I believe. I believe." Glen howled, wincing as Jim Bob squeezed his neck.

"Now, get outta here and remember what you promised here tonight," Jim Bob released Glen with a slight shove toward the door. The band had quit playing and the bar was quiet as a church during communion.

Glen shuffled toward the front door, his shoulders hunched over in contrition. Marcus thought he heard a sniffle from Glen, and he thought he saw Glen wipe a tear trickling down his left cheek.

Jim Bob turned toward Desiree. He cupped her hands in his massive paws and looked her tenderly in the eyes, "You OK?"

"You didn't have to do that, but thank you," Desiree hugged Jim Bob.

"No one goes after my friends without paying a price," Jim Bob said. Then realizing everyone was still watching the spectacle turned toward the band, "I thought there was a party going on around here? Where's the music?"

The drummer beat out the count with his sticks and the band broke into the swing that had been interrupted five minutes earlier.

Patti put her arm around Desiree and led her back to the booth. Jim Bob and Marcus followed.

"Friend, huh?" Marcus said, leaning toward Jim Bob, lightly bumping him shoulder to shoulder.

"Don't press your luck, Wind Woy," Jim Bob said looking straight ahead.

The four went back to the booth. Patti looked admiringly at Jim Bob. Oscar provided some ice wrapped in a bar towel for Desiree to hold against her injured eye, just in case. Marcus learned that Glenn had been obsessing over Desiree since high school. The obsession had escalated into stalking; hence, the restraining order. Desiree admitted that she had thought about leaving Williston for a fresh start somewhere far away, but that would just be running from her problem, and that wasn't like her.

Besides, her family had roots in Williston. Her grandfather was a successful farmer, her dad a CPA. They had oil on their land, and money now was no object. Desiree was the sole heir to all of it. She could go anywhere she wanted, but, "Williston is home," as she said. "I love my job helping babies get a healthy start in this world. Seeing the joy those babies bring to new parents and brothers and sisters just makes me feel so . . . so . . . so necessary," she said. "There's something so totally refreshing and hopeful about a newborn, don't you think?"

Marcus saw there was much more to Desiree than met the eye, and there was a lot to meet the eye. "I don't' even know your last name, and after that dance, I should at least know your last name," Marcus chuckled and turned to look Desiree in the face. The redness over the eye was fading, and Desiree had placed the ice rag on the table.

"Chambers. Desiree Chambers," she said

"You're sittin next to a local celebrity," Patti chimed.

"Patti, you know I don't like–"

"Oh, hush, Dee. I don't know why you're so self-conscious about it," Patti looked squarely at Marcus, "Dee here is a former Miss North Dakota and a Miss America third runner up. And in all the years we've been best friends, I've never ever seen her hit on a man," Patti paused, "until tonight."

"Well, that sounds like a compliment to me, Patti," Marcus's shy side showed up. He turned to Desiree, "Nice to meet you Desiree Chambers. I'm honored to have the company of such an accomplished woman," Marcus reached over and took Desiree's hand under the table.

"I apologize for acting so slutty. I don't know what

came over me."

"No offense taken, Desiree."

"Call me Dee."

Jim Bob cleared his throat, "If you two don't mind, I'm gonna take Patti home. Dee will you make sure Wind Boy here gets to where he's supposed to go? I gotta get him back to Tulsa tomorrow in one piece."

"I'll take good care of him," Desiree promised as she squeezed Marcus's hand.

Twenty minutes later Desiree pulled up to Marcus's hotel. Desiree made small talk during the trip, but Marcus sensed what she was hinting at.

"I watched your video," Desiree confessed without warning.

"What?" Marcus was surprised and puzzled.

"Your video. The speech. Patti told me about you, and I just Googled your name out of curiosity, and the You Tube video came up. Did you know it has nearly 2,000 views?" Desiree didn't give Marcus time to answer. "When I came to the bar tonight, I knew who you were, and I knew what I was doing. Your speech was so honest and tender. And I felt I knew who you were from what I saw coming through. I've seen a lot of fakes in my day, and you aren't one of them. I just hope I didn't make a fool out of myself. I'm ashamed of the way I rubbed myself against you. I'm really not that kind of girl."

"I uh . . . I uh . . . That's OK. I'd be less than honest if I didn't admit that I liked it." Desiree giggled quietly, suppressing it with her fingertips. Marcus went silent for a few seconds. "But I'm trying to figure out what 's happening with me and Anna right now. I hope you understand."

"I understand," Desiree said. "But if she isn't lovin' you every chance she gets by now, she's a fool."

Marcus looked for a way to change the subject, "What about you? It's hard to imagine that you aren't married by now, if that's what you want."

"I do want it, and believe me I've had offers. But mostly from men wanting a trophy wife to go along with their other expensive toys. I'm not that kind of girl, and I don't need to be kept, if you know what I mean."

"Yeah, I get it."

"Really? Do you know what it's like to have men visually grope you as you walk by and make sexual comments so you can hear them? They go on about how well endowed they are and how much pleasure they can give me. Makes me want to puke. Truth is more than likely they don't have a clue about how to pleasure a woman."

"I'm sorry. I didn't mean to—"

"No, I'm sorry to go off like that. It's just that . . . I thought I had found true love once, too," Desiree got quiet and turned more serious. "Back after the Miss America days, the local TV station was eager to have me on staff. I thought they saw some talent in me, but as it turned out I was just a pretty face, a temporary celebrity, with a great bod. I was just ratings to them. That's all. They didn't take me seriously. I thought one of the producers was in love with me. He was different from the locals, being from Chicago and all. More sophisticated, you know. It seemed like he knew me for who I was, not just the skin deep kind of beauty, but like he knew my heart," Desiree paused. Marcus wanted to ask questions, but kept quiet. "Anyway, he got an offer from the network, and he was gone. He said he would try to get me a shot at a Chicago station. Before that could happen, he was out on assignment covering some kind of gang violence or something. There was gunfire. As I understand the story, a stray bullet ricocheted off a brick wall and hit him in the head. And that was that."

"I'm sorry," Marcus sympathized. "I remember hearing something about that–like five or so years ago."

"Yeah, that was it. Bummer, huh?"

"Yeah, bummer."

"Anyway, I wasn't made for TV as it turned out. I finished my R-N degree and got a job at the medical center in Williston. Then the oil boom hit, and Williston went crazy. It won't last, you know. It never does. But, hey, we hit oil. Lots of it. But money can't buy love, huh?"

"I guess not," Marcus said.

Desiree suddenly reached across and clutched Marcus around the neck and pulled him over and kissed him hard at first, then when Marcus didn't resist, settled into a deep lingering kiss that ended with a soft separation as Desiree licked Marcus's lips tenderly. "So long, Wind Boy. If the Anna thing doesn't work out, you know where to find me."

"I hope you find what you're looking for. I'm glad you told me all this. You're even more beautiful than when I first saw you tonight." Marcus opened the car door and got out. Then leaning in, "I won't forget this night, or you. Ever."

Marcus flipped the lamp on as he entered his room. He tossed the contents of his pockets on the nightstand and checked his phone. Still no messages. He took off his shirt and t-shirt and sat down to unlace his boots and placed them to the side of the chair. Marcus sat quietly, reflecting on all that had happened the past three hours. He leaned back in the chair resting his head on the high upholstered back.

Desiree is without question the sexiest woman I've

ever met. I wish I had the words to tell her how deeply beautiful she is. Wow, how first impressions can be so wrong. I thought she was just some hot, dingy local girl looking for another good time with her best girlfriend and her boyfriend from out of town. Yeah, Anna is beautiful and all those things, but she has never touched me with the tenderness that Desiree did. And yeah, I've hugged Anna, and we have cuddled, sort of, but there's always an edge to her, like she is afraid of getting close. But Desiree? GAWWWWWWWWWD. I will never ever forget that dance. That was the gold standard of sexy, sultry, slow dances. The kind you see in the movies, and know you'll probably never have. I know I did the right thing by not letting this night go too far. Will Anna ever show me that kind of affection and tenderness that I thought she would when we first met?

Then there's Jim Bob. What a surprise. What a teddy bear—the teddy bear torpedo. Marcus chuckled out loud to himself sitting there in the hotel room alone with his eyes closed and head leaned back holding the picture of Jim Bob manhandling and humiliating Glen then nestling up to Patti. *He definitely is into Patti. I can see it in that stupid grin of his. The way his eyes squint when he talks and especially when he smiles. Don't worry, Jim Bob. I won't tell anyone about that soft side. Your hard ass image is safe with me. There has been a bucket load of surprises on this trip.*

Marcus could feel his eyes getting that drowsy feeling. A soft but rapid knock on the door aroused him. He stood up and hastily slipped into his shirt that he had tossed onto the foot of the bed. Marcus walked barefoot into the entry without turning on any more lights. He leaned over and looked through the peephole, then, opened the door.

He had barely cracked the door when Desiree stepped through, pushing it the rest of the way open. As she passed Marcus, she paused briefly and placed the palm of her hand on his bare chest, exposed by the unbuttoned shirt, and glanced up at him. Marcus stood silently, looking into Desiree's dark eyes. Her touch was warm and soothing . . . and welcome. She let it linger for a moment then allowed her fingertips to slide across Marcus's abs as she strolled into the room and dropped her handbag onto the bed. Desiree turned to face Marcus, shifting her weight onto her left leg and placing her left hand on her waist, said, "I'm not a fool."

Marcus let the door close behind him.

5. X-factor

Elliot Sloan leafed through the pages of the *Tulsa World*, sipping coffee at a patio table outside Hemingway's on Cherry Street as Marcus approached. Elliot always exuded an air of casual self-assurance. Marcus envied that quality. *It must be comforting to know that you don't have to prove anything to anyone,* Marcus grinned at the scene. Elliot had become his valued mentor at Johnstone Enterprises.

Elliot noticed Marcus and stood, "Marcus, my man," he gathered Marcus into a bro hug, something that had never happened before.

"Hey, Elliot. This is new," Marcus reacted. "What's this all about?"

"Well, you made it through four days with Jim Bob, and from what I hear, managed to make a good impression on the rig crews. That puts you in the club, as far as I'm concerned," Elliot chuckled.

"It was definitely an interesting week," Marcus replied.

"What would you say was your biggest takeaway from the trip?" Elliot asked as a waiter approached just as Marcus took his seat.

Marcus addressed the waiter before answering Elliot, "I'll have lemon ginger tea and a mixed berry scone." The waiter acknowledged the order. "Well, my biggest takeaway, other than how much food a roughneck can pack away, was how intense some of the crews were. There's no margin for error on the rig, or someone can get hurt."

"How did you get along with Jim Bob?"

"Well, we got off to a rocky start, but I think we were getting along OK by the time we left. No doubt Jim Bob is highly regarded for his expertise. But, you know, I could never get away with talking to my team the way he went after some of the guys in the field. I was really uncomfortable a couple of times listening to him berate a toolpusher."

"Yeah, that's a big knock on Jim Bob, and he's not likely to change," Elliot admitted. "But he can get a drill bit dead on where it needs to be."

"It's just a different culture out there. I guess everyone just accepts it. I casually mentioned it to Jim Bob, you know, that he was sure hard on a guy. He said there was nothing like a good ass chewing for motivation."

"Yeah, the reason they made him a consultant is so he doesn't directly supervise anyone. His boss, Aaron, has to read him the riot act every once in a while. Word gets back. But somehow the drilling gets better after he's in the field. Darnedest thing."

"Well, he wasn't hard on everyone. I did meet a couple of hands that he thought highly of. But he didn't exactly lavish them with praise," Marcus observed. "What do you think his future is at Johnstone?"

"He's pretty much topped out. He contributes where he is, but he's not management or leadership material. I get the impression he's not the least bit interested in it either."

"No doubt he loves being on the rigs," Marcus said, then pivoted. "Jim Bob said something at the airport Monday morning that has caused me to wonder, and I'd like to ask you about it."

"OK." Elliot paused to sip his newly refreshed coffee.

"He said he was surprised that I was on the corporate jet and that he expected me to take a commercial flight up. All I know is that I got word from Mr. Johnstone's office to show up at the hanger. Is that unusual? And if it is, is that kind of treatment going to be a problem for me?"

"How do you mean?" Elliot probed.

"I mean, Mr. Johnstone has been very kind to me, and I'm worried that his favor can come with a price in the eyes of others around the company."

"I know Nelson pretty well, and the one thing I can tell you is he makes business decisions," Elliot said emphatically. "What else do you think putting you on that flight could mean? Put yourself in Nelson's chair as CEO."

Marcus took a bite of his scone and sipped his tea while he took a moment to think. "Well, he could be sending a signal that he thinks what we are doing at Millennium is as important as what oil and gas is doing. That we're equal in some ways. That Millennium belongs along side oil and gas."

"Yeah. That would make sense," Elliot agreed.

"So it wasn't just singling me out as a favorite or anything like that."

"Like I said, Nelson makes business decisions," Elliot repeated. "In Nelson's mind, you belonged on that flight just like anyone else. I know Elliot was impressed that you offered to take vacation days to make that trip."

"Yes, that I did," Marcus admitted. "I thought it would be easier to get approval for the trip that way, for some reason."

"What it showed, Marcus, was initiative to get outside your own world and understand the world of oil and gas. As the VP of drilling, Aaron wanted your lab space if Millennium lost funding. Regardless, when word got to him about your request, it was Aaron who suggested putting you on that flight. That's a hell of a compliment."

"I guess I didn't realize all that, Elliot."

"Marcus, leaders take the initiative to make things better. Leaders step up to change the status quo when it needs to be changed. Can you ever conceive of Jim Bob reaching out to you to make things better?"

"No, not really."

"That's the difference between you and Jim Bob. You are both very talented and skilled. But you possess an X-factor that sets you apart."

"An X-factor?" Marcus asked. "That sounds like a super hero something or other . . . uh, I'm not that kind of a guy. No super powers or anything," Marcus hedged, chuckling at the thought.

"No, it's not a super power, but it is rare. Marcus, you have a quality about you that when you face a challenge, you don't back down, and you work through it. Even more, you bring those on your team along with you. You help them through the change and make them better for the experience. That's the X-factor that few people have. I believe Nelson thinks that by using you as an example, those qualities can spread to other leaders and those who want to become leaders."

"That's very flattering. I just try to do what I think is right. I know I have a long way to go to be a great leader, but I'm willing to learn, and to push myself," Marcus said.

"I call that maturing, Marcus. What does that word mean to you—maturing?" Elliot continued.

"I know to my dad it meant getting out on my own

and becoming a tax-paying citizen," Marcus chuckled at the example.

"That's part of it," Elliot agreed echoing the chuckle. "And more. Your dad wanted you to become self-supporting and self-directed. That meant you could be on your own and he wouldn't have to worry about you. Right?"

"Yeah, I guess that's a better way to put it. Along the way he would tell me when I was getting off track, or needed to improve. Sometimes my oldest sister, Lauren, thought she needed to set me straight. She kind of still does."

"Erin recognized that you reached a certain level of maturity as an engineer. She thought you had the makings of an effective supervisor and promoted you," Elliot explained. "But when you moved into that position, you also took a step backward in job maturity."

"Ok, I'm not sure I follow," Marcus was curious.

"The maturity cycle says that you reach a certain level of maturity where you are self-directed and self-supporting. Then, you step up to a higher level that's new to you, and you have to learn how to become self-directed and self-supporting in that new role or that new environment. As a supervisor, you are learning to improve your leadership abilities, and someday, you will probably step up to another role requiring higher talents, and the maturing process starts all over. We are always learning, changing, and growing. Evolving, so to speak. Those who cannot, or will not, adapt will top out at a lower level."

"Sort of like being promoted to your level of incompetence," Marcus chuckled.

"Yeah, kind of like that," Elliot echoed the chuckle, "and we all know people like that because they didn't continue to grow and develop."

"I see that now. Like Sue Ann wanting to handle that project debrief a couple of months ago. She called it a growth opportunity for her," Marcus said.

"You recognized how important it was to Sue Ann instead of shutting her down. That shows you are growing, too. Putting you on that flight was a way for Aaron and Nelson to put you in a position to grow more from that experience. If they are going to build a leadership course around your ideas, you have to be seen as someone who leads by example. That's an X-factor they see in you. And becoming mature will mean that you can see the X-factors in others and help them build those into personal strengths." Elliot paused to let the message seep in.

"I guess I never thought of it that way," Marcus leaned back and ran the fingers of his left hand through his hair.

"Tell me, Marcus, did you see Jim Bob actually coach any of the hands about how they could do a better job?" Elliot asked.

"I can't say that I did," Marcus answered slowly, imagining back at the scenes of Jim Bob on the rigs. "Mostly he just told them that he knew what he was doing, that he had put more holes in the ground and hit more oil and

"We are always learning, changing, and growing. Evolving. Those who cannot, or will not, adapt will top out at a lower level."

gas than all of them combined. If they couldn't do it the way he told them, they'd find someone who could. That kind of stuff," Marcus reported.

"Well, that's why Jim Bob doesn't run a crew day to day. And Aaron tries to get it through that thick skull of his that he needs to change his ways. It's got to be tough being Jim Bob," Elliot shook his head in bemusement. "Maybe you'll rub off on him."

"I'm not sure I'll be spending that much time with Jim Bob," Marcus quickly added. Then he paused a moment and asked, "So, you think I have what it takes? You really believe I can be that guy?" Marcus questioned.

"Yes. Yes I do, Marcus. It means that evolutionary change is not enough though."

"So, what will it take?"

"It will take transformational change," Elliot stated.

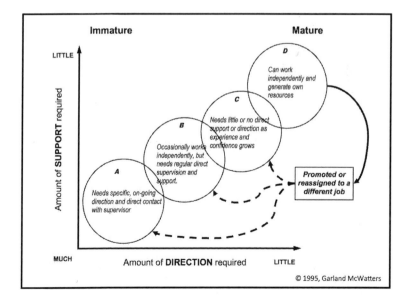

EVOLUTIONARY change is a natural progression of change, such as aging.

REVOLUTIONARY change is a disruptive upheaval.

TRANSFORMATIONAL change is reshaping or reinventing something into a fundamentally different state or condition, hopefully for the better.

"What's the difference?" Marcus asked.

"Evolutionary change is the natural change that comes with the flow of life, like aging. Transformational change is reinventing yourself to see yourself and think of yourself in different ways. That's a change that changes your identity—a caterpillar to a butterfly kind of change. That's where I think you are headed. That's why I'm spending this time with you. I want to be close by as it's happening." Elliot reached out and put his hand on Marcus's shoulder. "That's why I couldn't resist the bro hug," Elliot blurted out a hearty laugh, and Marcus joined in.

"Your mentoring and friendship mean a lot to me, Elliot. Promise you'll always be straight with me when I need it."

"Well, I'm not here to make you in my image or to be a surrogate dad. I hope I can help you find your path as you seek it out and point you to others who can help out too."

"Like Amy Capshaw?" Marcus said.

"Exactly. Like Amy Capshaw. She's a pro, and I hope you will treasure her advice and coaching."

"I could not have made that presentation at the company retreat without her. It would have been a disaster. Speaking of speaking, I got a call from one of Lizzie's friends, Pete, who I met at her cookout. He invited me to speak to their supervisors at the end of July. Do you think I'm ready for something like that?" Marcus asked.

"What do you think?" Elliot replied.

"I would like to give it a try. I really enjoyed the public speaking, and I think it's something I could grow into," Marcus admitted.

"Sounds transformational to me," Elliot approved.

6. Risky business

His mentoring session with Elliot had been on Marcus's mind all week. Thinking about it caused him to be more self-aware about the conversations he had with his team members. Several times, when he was deep into one of his tasks, a tech asked him for advice. He put down what he was doing and took time to hear their questions and lead them through finding a solution or coming up with something different to try. He was reflecting on one of those conversations when Whitney Ellis called. He answered immediately, "Hey, Whitney, how are you doing?" Marcus began.

"Pretty OK. Got a minute?"

"Sure. What can I do for you?"

"Just a couple of things. First, I wanted to find out what you thought about our meet up group and if you are planning to come to the next lunch."

"Yeah. Actually I enjoyed the conversation. It made me realize that we all face similar situations regardless of what industry we work in. Will it be at Miguel's again?"

"Yep. Same place, same time. Abby also has a Facebook page up for the group. Did you see the email about it?"

"Yeah, but I haven't linked up to it yet. I guess I should, huh," Marcus admitted. "But anyway, I do plan to be there, and be on time this time."

"Good," Whitney chirped. "Now for my second thing. I have a situation I wanted to bounce off you. Can you spare a few minutes?"

"Sure. What's up?"

"It's about our new billing system I told you about. We are just floundering with the change over, and I can't get any of my managers to buy into more training for our associates. I'm at a loss, and I was hoping that you might have some ideas," Whitney sounded exasperated.

"Why do you think your managers are so resistant to the idea?" Marcus asked.

"Well, I'm just one of nine account managers, and I'm the youngest. I just don't think they respect me or believe that what I'm saying is true. My boss just gets annoyed at me and tells me the other account managers are handling it. He said I just need to motivate my associates and get them to try harder."

"How are the other account managers handling it?" Marcus pushed.

"They're really not. They are barely hanging on with their volume and deadlines. The turnover is high on their teams. It's hard enough to keep new employees, and now some of the veterans are leaving, too."

"Why do you think training is the answer?" Marcus continued.

"I would say that new employees start the job highly motivated to do a good job. The old system was a lot easier. Everyone seems to catch on quickly. We still have a lot of our client files in that system. Right now we're going back and forth between the two systems. The full migration is going to happen over the Fourth of July weekend. They just don't know how to do their job, and the tools aren't working right. Yet, they are expected to turn out as much volume as before. I can't do anything about the software, but I think I can help with training them on the new system faster," Whitney explained.

"And your managers aren't aware of the problems?" Marcus asked.

"They said they learned on the job and figured stuff out when they started and don't see why our associates can't do the same thing," Whitney said. "Just because they did that job several years ago doesn't mean it's the same job now. Things have changed. It's more complex, and we're handling ten times the clients they handled back then."

"Well, Whitney, it sounds like you've tried to explain it to them, but they aren't buying it. What else could you do?" Marcus asked.

"I think I can put together a simple training series using screen shots and narrating a brief explanation and just make it available someway."

"Will management see that as going against their wishes?" Marcus wondered.

"I can stay late and do a couple each night. I already have a list of the top ten issues I hear the most about. By the end of the week I think I can have enough done to deal with seventy-five percent of the issues. I think if my managers see it work and the production improves, they'll take it more seriously. The vendor doesn't offer any meaningful training, as it turns out, and I'm willing to take the risk," Whitney said.

"I agree. I think if you can show them a payoff you might get more buy in. I mean, who can argue with better productivity or higher morale? Right?" Marcus sounded encouraging. "If I were in your place, I'd probably do the same kind of thing."

"I appreciate the encouragement. I just can't see why some people would just keep banging their head on a brick wall instead of making the obvious changes?"

"In this case, Whitney, your associates are more directly impacted by the system and the demands than the managers are. Where do you think you have the best chance to make a difference?" Marcus asked.

"With my associates," Whitney replied instantly.

"Then, focus on what your associates are telling you, and help them solve their problem. I'm sure they will appreciate your solution even if the managers are slower to come around," Marcus said.

"What if my supervisor thinks I'm being insubordinate? Do you think I'll really get in trouble?

"That's always a risk. Change is risky, and change makers are risk takers. The question is whether you are willing to take the risk."

"I'd rather be damned for doing than damned for not, but that's just me—a little hell raiser," Whitney said.

4 things all employees want to know from their supervisor:

1. **WHAT** do you want me to do?

2. **HOW** do you want me to do it?

3. **Am I OK?**

4. **How will you HELP me?**

"It sounds like you've pretty much decicedd, then," Marcus concluded.

"Yep. I guess so. Thanks for listening," Whitney said.

"One more thing, Whitney. This year I learned some questions I always keep in mind as I think about my team. I tell myself that they are always needing to know the answer to these questions, and it's my job to know the answer," Marcus offered.

"I'd love to know what those are," Whitney was curious.

"Here goes. Let me know when you are ready."

Whiney paused, "I've got something to write with. Go ahead."

"OK. First, what do you want me to do? That's the goal, the end result. You need to be absolutely clear about it. No double signals."

"Tell me about it," Whitney added. "I probably should ask my supervisor exactly what he expects out of me. I feel like I'm trying by hardest, but I'm not sure if I'm right on target."

"Yeah. Wouldn't hurt to double check. Second question. How do you want me to do it? That's about process and quality standards. That's how you know whether the work is being done to expectations."

"Never thought of that one, Marcus. How many times do we just assume everyone knows what those standards are?"

"Tell me. I've learned to make sure we are clear about the standards," Marcus added. "Third. And this one is really important. Am I OK? Everyone needs assurance that their job is safe and they are in good standing with you."

"I need to ask that one myself, but I don't want to sound needy and insecure," Whitney said.

"It doesn't have to come across that way," Marcus explained. "You can say something like you just want to make sure you are doing what's expected and you want to get clear about the outcomes and how they will be evaluated. That way it sounds like you are trying to be a problem solver."

"I see what you mean. I can even preface my instructions to my team by sayhing I want to make sure they are OK with the changes, and we need to go over the new process and make sure we are doing it correctly."

"That's the idea. Here's the fourth question. How will you help me? Our job as supervisors is to help our team be successful and confident. You do those four things for your team, and I'm sure you'll get their buy in. It's worked for me," Marcus as-sured.

"That makes a lot of sense to me, Marcus. I'll try it right away. Maybe I'll have something positive to report at lunch next week," Whitney sounded optimistic.

"I'll be eager to hear. Change is easier when people know exactly what's ex-pected, when they believe they can pull it off, and when they know you are there for them," Marcus concluded.

"I'll sure let you know. I think this will work for me. Thanks again, Marcus. See you Thursday."

"Sure thing. Later."

Marcus leaned back in his chair and gazed out his office window. Desiree Chambers had also been on his mind all week.

I don't know how to feel about what happened. On the one hand I feel . . . Marcus paused several seconds looking for the right word . . . *ashamed? Or, I think I should feel ashamed. But that doesn't seem like the right word. I'm single and I'm not in a sexual relationship with Anna, although I had hoped to be by now. Desiree made me come alive, and I did not realize how emotionally numb I had grown pursuing Anna.*

Am I off base to feel suspicious that Anna could have something going with Greer? I know Anna has a lot on her mind and all, and after what she said about her experience at A&M, it kind of makes sense why she would be cautious. Maybe it's her way of saying she's unsure of her feelings about me. Maybe it's just Anna. Maybe she isn't capable of being as affectionate as Desiree was. Anna and I talked briefly Sunday, and even then she was burning the candle at both ends between work and the campaign. She was barely interested in my trip. Mostly wanted to know if Jim Bob was a jerk. I told her I got to see another side of him, but no way did I tell her about the bar incident.

I'm sure Desiree is under no illusions that Wednesday night was anything other than what it was. She didn't ask for my phone number or email and didn't offer hers. Still, if she wanted to, I'm sure she'd have no trouble getting in touch, and wouldn't hesitate to reach out. But it's been soooooooo long since I've been touched the way Desiree touched me. And I didn't realize until that dance how starved I was for . . . Marcus signed deeply as he gazed out his office window. *This is crazy, Marcus. You'll never see or hear from Desiree again, and you would be double stupid if you tried to contact her, so drop it.*

Marcus stood up and stretched, standing on his tiptoes and raising his hands as high above his head as he could. He rolled his neck and shoulders and decided to head for the break area and brew a cup of tea. *Still, I'll never forget Desiree and all that happened. One of those moments that I didn't ask for–that I didn't initiate–but didn't resist either. Does that make me an asshole? I can still feel the way she pressed against me and how she felt in my embrace. The way it felt to fall asleep with her head on my shoulder. I never knew when she left and didn't get to say goodbye. Why can't I have that with Anna? Why won't Anna give herself to me? Maybe she will loosen up when I see her over the Fourth of July. One thing for sure, I know I'm ready and hungry for a loving relationship. Why, oh why, Anna, can't it be you? I want it to be with you. But I can't wait much longer.*

7. Independence Day

As Independence Day parades go, Springfield's is an extravaganza. Springfield citizens deck out the town in red, white, and blue bunting, and Old Glory flies in just about every yard. Marcus swelled with pride to be an American when the floats carrying military veterans passed. He stood a little straighter in respectful attention.

Marcus used the Fourth of July as an excuse to lavish extra attention on Susie and Andy, his niece and nephew. Lauren and Jarod indulged Marcus to buy double-dip ice cream cones and any holiday junk food they desired.

"Will we see Anna in the parade, Uncle Mark?" Andy asked. "Do you think she'll notice us?"

Eric Greer's congressional campaign had an entry. Anna, and a small entourage of staff and supporters would be walking with Greer, carrying signs and tossing candy into the throngs of eager children lining the streets.

"I'm sure she will," Susie replied. "You did tell Anna where to look for us, didn't you, Uncle Mark?" Susie asked tugging on Marcus's arm.

"Yeah, sure, Susie. I told her where we always stand. I think she'll see us," Marcus assured.

"I'll make sure, Uncle Mark," Andy said. "I'll step out and wave and shout at her."

"That ought to do it," Marcus smiled.

Lauren turned to Marcus, "I guess Anna's still coming over for dinner and the fireworks?" she asked.

"Yeah, this morning she said she was still on."

"Good," Lauren replied. "I've also invited Jeannie and Johnny. You know Jeannie likes to see you when you're here, and she doesn't see Anna as much any more either."

"We might see her up and down the parade route," Marcus added. "She called the other night to see if I was coming up, and she told me she wanted to take crowd shots at the parade now that she's got this awesome camera."

"You and Anna have been such a positive influence on her. I think back on that day when you just happened across her beside the lake. You never know what impact a simple casual meeting will have on the rest of your life. Do you?" Lauren observed.

"Life is full of changes and surprises, for sure," Marcus agreed.

"For sure," Lauren smiled. "I see her a couple of times a week. The change in her has been—" Lauren hesitated, "Remarkable. She's blossoming into a woman right before our eyes."

"Look," Andy shouted, pointing down the crowd-packed street, "the parade's here."

Group by group paraded by. The types of entries were the same from year to year. Scout groups, veterans groups, the police department, the Greene County sheriff's department, firefighters, the U.S. Army Reserve unit, various churches, civic groups, the Missouri State University rodeo club, and other riding clubs from southwest Missouri. The Shriners driving go-carts and other vehicles in precision routines were always a crowd pleaser.

Incumbent politicians and dignitaries waived from the backseats of chauffeured vintage cars supplied by the car club. Preston Collins, the first-term congressman for Missouri's fourth congressional district, rode on a blue 1969 Camero Supersport convertible with his two preschool grandchildren perched on either side of him. *Sweet ride,* Marcus thought. Greer was challenging Collins in the general election. Neither drew a primary opponent.

Eric Greer, leading his supporters, walked directly behind the band. The group of fifteen adults and another dozen children and teens all were dressed in blue t-shirts with the phrase "Go With Greer" on both the front and back. One elderly gentleman drove his electric wheelchair with American flags streaming above it. Two young uniformed war veterans in wheel chairs supporting Greer, both paraplegics, got standing ovations as they passed.

Anna walked at the back of the pack along Marcus's side of the street. She signaled that she saw Andy when he jumped out on the edge of the crowd and waived his arms over his head, "Anna! Anna!" he shouted. Anna stopped for a split second when she reached him.

"Here," she bent over to Andy and placed a hand full of candy in his palm. Then, looking up at Marcus she flashed a smile, "See you later," and kept moving.

Since Marcus was also watching for Anna first, he almost missed Greer. *Looks a little heavier than I expected,* Marcus thought as Greer passed. Greer wore a pale blue shirt, sleeves rolled up, and khaki slacks. He was on the far side of the street when he passed Marcus, then crisscrossed back over afterward, looking very energetic and shaking hands, high-fiving, and fist-bumping. Well, I guess I'll get a better look Saturday when I go to his rally with Anna.

* * *

Jarod handed Marcus a beer. They sat on the veranda of Jarod and Lauren's home. A ceiling fan circulated the warm late afternoon air. Lauren, Susie and Adam set plates, cups, and flatware on the serving table. Family and guests would be arriving soon. Marcus's phone chimed. He did not recognize the number on the caller ID, but it was a 918 area code. Tulsa.

"Hello, this is Marcus."

A female voice responded, "Marcus Winn?"

"Yes."

"Marcus, forgive the call on a holiday. I'm Valerie Kirk with Congressman Wakefield's office."

Marcus stood, motioning to Jarod that he needed to take the call, "Hi, yeah, I'm surprised to hear from you on a holiday." Marcus strolled into the yard where he could have some privacy.

"Yeah, it's a 24-7 type job. Marcus, the congressman is in Tulsa for the weekend. He had a cancellation in his schedule tomorrow morning and wondered if you were available for a meeting. I know this is sooner than we had discussed, but the congressman is very interested in what you have to say about renewable energy."

"I'm sorry, but I'm out of state for the weekend," Marcus answered.

"We were just hoping," Valerie paused, "I'll tell the congressman. We'll stick with our original timeline. Have a nice weekend, then, and thank you."

"Sorry I'm not available, but thanks for asking."

"We'll be in touch soon," Valerie ended the call.

"Hope it wasn't bad news," Jarod said as Marcus strolled back onto the ve-randa.

"No, just an update on a project I'm involved with. "

"Seems like projects don't respect holidays, do they?"

Jarod chuckled.

"Some things never change."

"You got that right," Jarod lifted his bottle in agreement. "From what Lauren says, it sounds like you are getting a lot of attention at your company. We both saw the video of your speech, you know."

"I hope you didn't mind the personal references."

"Not at all. We wondered why you were so intense on that line of questioning back in October. Now it all makes sense," Jarod said.

"I was having a bad day when I arrived for that weekend, but things worked out," Marcus mused.

"We thought there was something going on, but we had no idea what. But, hey, if you hadn't been hit with that crisis, you wouldn't be where you are today. You know, a celebrity, jetting around in the corporate jet, rubbing shoulders with billionaires, that kind of thing."

"I guess I never thought of it like that," Marcus paused, "I was just so fixed on surviving that I haven't stopped to think about all that."

"Yeah, I kind of went through a phase like that when I stepped up to COO of our business. Before that I was just the boss's kid. Then as I learned the business more and started making a difference, people began treating me a little differently—more seriously. I was getting invited to business planning meetings around town. People were asking me what I thought. Even got a couple of encouraging words to run for the state legislature. I thought, why would I want to do that? What would I have to offer? I'm no politician. Flattering, but not for me." Marcus had never heard this from his brother-in-law.

"You might be selling yourself short, bro. You've got a lot to offer."

"Not my scene Markie, not my scene."

"Looking back I can see how I've changed since October. But I wasn't aware of it while it was happening," Marcus said.

"Yeah? Like what?"

"Well, for one thing I'm a lot more aware of what my team is doing. I talk to them more about their work, and I ask their ideas more often. I realize how much of a loner I was before Theresa insisted that I meet more people at work. I would never have thought that I would like public speaking as much as I do, and how naturally it comes to me. I felt like I was really connecting with the audience, and I would not have called myself a storyteller," Marcus explained.

"Those are all good things, Marcus. And they all came out of whatever you were dealing with at the time," Jarod observed.

"Some of them were pretty stressful. I just did what I had to."

"I've heard that the stress zone is the learning zone," Jarod added. "You never know what you can do and how hard you will push yourself until you have to, or else."

"You got that right," Marcus chuckled, raising his bottle in agreement.

"Some change happens naturally as a part of living. We evolve. Other change is forced on us by events, like a revolution. We tend to push back at first, get defensive. Then we get our head on straight and figure out what we have to do to get through it," Jarod summarized.

Both paused for another sip.

"Who's Theresa?" Jarod asked, "I don't think I've heard you mention her before."

"Theresa. Oh, yeah, Theresa. I guess I haven't men-

The STRESS ZONE

is the

LEARNING ZONE

You never know how hard you are willing to push yourself to change until you have to, or else.

tioned her. She's a friend at work who has been introducing me around her side of the company. We met casually one day and struck up a friendship."

"Does Anna know her?"

"No, but she knows about her. No big deal," Marcus took another sip to break eye contact with Jarod. "Speaking of getting through it," Marcus changed the subject, "what do you know about this Eric Greer guy that Anna is working for?"

"I've seen him around, but I don't know him personally. I don't hear any big negatives—except that he's a Democrat," Jarod chuckled, tipping the mouth of his bottle toward Marcus, then backtracked, "Not a bleeding heart though."

"I would think anyone from Missouri would be pretty practical. You know, we're the showme state," Marcus said.

"You'll get a closer look Saturday at his rally."

"Yeah, I promised Anna I would hang around for it. She thinks I'll like him and see why she's so high on him," Marcus didn't sound as if he was looking forward to the encounter.

"Lauren and I are not very political, but we have not been impressed with Collins. He came in on that anti-Washington change everything wave, and it was an open seat. I think Greer will make it a close race regardless," Jarod explained.

The back door flung open, Andy burst out, "Anna's here. Anna's here, Uncle Mark. Anna's here."

"OK, OK, OK, I'm on my way," Marcus rose up slowly from the rattan chair, took Jarod's bottle with his and deposited them in the recycle tub on his way into the house.

Marcus stepped through the back door into the kitchen, then, stopped in his tracks when he saw Anna, her back to him, emptying a grocery sack of various chips and snacks at the kitchen island as Andy crowded up next to her offering to help. She had shed her parade uniform of jeans and a "Go with Greer" t-shirt for a pair of navy blue shorts, sandals, and a white blouse with tiny red dots sprinkled around the fabric. Her straight hair came to a V between her shoulder blades. Her toned and tanned arms and legs highlighted against the white island and cabinets in the back-ground.

Lauren's voice intruded into his spontaneous trance, "Marcus, hon, will you tell Jarod it's time to get the grill ready?"

Anna turned from her chore, "Marcus," a wide smile–the kind you can't fake–spread as she scurried to him, embracing him around the neck and planting a kiss on his left cheek. "I'm so happy to finally be here."

Marcus hugged her, pulling her tightly against his chest, relishing the moment. It had been weeks since he last held her. He was hungry for her. But he turned loose before the scene became awkward. "I miss you so much," he whispered as he loosened his embrace.

"Me, too," Anna whispered back.

The front door opened. Andy and Susie turned toward the foyer. "J-Ma, Pappy," Andy yelled as he ran to greet Jarod's parents, Jacqueline and Jon Holman.

Everyone in the kitchen stopped in mid task and turned. Emily, Marcus's sister, and Owen, her husband, entered next followed by Andrew and Melanie Winn, Marcus's father and mother.

"Granddad, Memaw," Andy exclaimed.

Marcus bounded into the family room and grabbed Emily up in a hug, reaching out to shake Owen's hand without releasing Emily, "Man, it's so good to see you. How long can you stay?" Marcus asked.

"Have to head back Friday morning," Emily explained. "Owen works Saturday at the clinic." Emily spotted Anna standing in the entry to the kitchen, "And this must be Anna?"

Marcus reached out to Anna, a gesture for her to join him, "Yes . . .yes." Anna entered as Marcus placed his hand in the small of her back, "May I present, officially, AnnaMarie Flores. Anna, this is my sister Emily Mize, and her husband, Owen."

Emily offered her hand, "A pleasure to meet you, finally. I've heard a lot about you from everyone."

"My pleasure as well, " Anna replied

Lauren made her way through the hugs to greet her sister and brother-in-law. She caught her mother's eye and noticed a grin about to break out, Melanie glanced at

Emily, who also was suppressing a similar grin. "What?" Lauren asked, looking back and forth between Emily and her mother.

"We're pregnant," Emily squealed with delight, "we're pregnant, finally."

"That's wonderful, Sis," Marcus went for another hug, "I won't squeeze so tight this time.."

"I'm so happy for you. How long have you known?" Lauren looked at her mother like she had been keeping secrets, "Mother?"

"Don't look at me," Melanie held her palms up to fend off the implied accusation. "We just found out this morning when they drove in."

"When are you due?" Lauren asked

"Early February. The third or fourth, as close as we can tell."

"Well, there'll be some changes at your place, won't there?" Marcus said.

"We have so much to do," Emily said

"She's got a list," Owen chimed in. "A very long list."

"This is one change I've dreamed of for so long," Emily beamed.

Lauren and Marcus gathered Emily up in a group hug.

"OK, Marcus. You're next up," Owen chided. "No pressure though."

"Well, pretty sure that's not in my immediate plans," Marcus resisted the urge to look at Anna.

By five-o'clock the veranda was almost set with tables draped in a traditional red and white checked tablecloth. Jarod and Marcus had put the finishing touches on the stars and stripes bunting draped from the edges of the veranda's framing. Andrew and Jon were talking shop under the veranda's cool mist fans mounted in the corners above their favorite patio swivel gliders, cold brew in hand. The aroma of freshly baked apple pie drifted from the kitchen. Lauren was about to bring it out to the dessert table. Marcus stepped back to take in the scene. *This is as close to perfect as it gets. I don't know what more I can hope for right now, except, maybe, for Anna to finally say it's time for us to go to the next level.*

"Jeannie," Andy shouted out when he saw Jeannie and Johnny, turn off the lake trail and start up the expansive back yard. He dropped his sketch pad and dashed to meet her, falling in step beside her. Andy took two steps to each of Jeannie's long, slow strides, which were made to look simultaneously elegant and sensuous by her blue spandex shorts beneath a red and white vertical striped spaghetti strap top. Her deep red hair, usually in a ponytail or bun, today cascaded over her shoulders and down her back. With both hands, she carried a gallon sized serving bowl containing what looked like a dessert. As she glided, the bowl swayed side to side in perfect syncopation with her hips and gait. Her bright red lipstick perfectly matched the frames of her sunglasses. To her left, Johnny carried her camera bag like an obedient boy servant.

Marcus scampered to meet her midway into the yard. He reached out to take the dish. Jeannie flashed a bashful smile letting Marcus take the bowl. "Why Marcus Winn, thank you. You are such a gentleman to come lift my burden," Jeannie played the coy southern belle, letting Marcus take the bowl. "Banana pudding. My dad's favorite. Who doesn't like banana pudding? Right?"

"Right," Marcus stammered. "Uh, you look, uh, you look patriotic," was the safest word that came to mind when he was thinking *drop dead gorgeous*. "Looks like you've been getting some sun, too."

"I wish I could actually tan. This barely beige tone is about as good as it's gonna get, I'm afraid."

"Well, you look great."

"Thanks," Jeannie dropped the southern belle act. "I've been looking forward to this evening. I love being around your family. It's the best thing that's happened to me in years." Jeannie mussed Andy's hair as the group fell into step toward the house.

"Did you get any good pictures at the parade today?" Marcus asked.

"Mostly crowd shots and some candids where the parade was assembling."

"I look forward to seeing what you got."

"I look forward to showing you," Jeannie flashed that coy grin again.

Marcus paused briefly, "Well, then, let's get this dessert to the table." Marcus looked down at his nephew who had not given up his place on Jeannie's right hip.

"Can we get in our customary walk around the lake in the morning? I hate to miss my chance to have you to myself," Jeannie asked as they walked toward the house.

"For sure. Can you go early while it's still cool?"

"As early as you want."

"How about 8:30 then?"

"I'll meet you at the bench."

"All right. I'll be there."

Susie and Anna stood at the edge of the veranda as Jeannie's entourage approached. Susie took charge of Johnny. Anna stepped off the veranda to hug Jeannie.

"Jeannie, you look amazing," Anna exclaimed. "Look at you. You are blossoming. You look radiant."

"Thanks to you and Marcus, I've got a lot going that I didn't have several months ago," Jeannie beamed, glancing back and forth between Anna and Marcus as she spoke.

"I guess you got settled in with Christine?"

Marcus had not heard this news. "So, who's Christine? What's going on?"

Anna explained, "Christine is a young widow I introduced to Jeannie, knowing Jeannie was looking to move out from her mother's house."

Jeannie picked up from there, "It's going great. We get along fantastic. I feel so totally at home. She lets me drive her second car like it's my own. It's perfect for me right now."

"I'm glad it's working out. Change can be stressful, and trying to make it on your own makes it harder. When people can help each other, things are usually easier," Anna offered.

"This is the best Fourth of July I can ever remember having," Jeannie had removed her sunglasses, and Marcus noticed her emerald eyes redden a little.

Anna hugged her, "I know how you feel."

Marcus sat the pudding on the dessert table, leaving Anna and Jeannie standing together chatting.

"Hey everyone," Jarod's voice rose above the crowd that had moved onto the veranda. "Welcome to the Holman Independence Day family picnic. We have three additions this year, and one on the way. Anna, Jeannie, Johnny, welcome to the family. Congratulations to Emily and Owen. Once you're in, you're in. That's the way it works in this clan. You have enriched our lives, so let's celebrate our freedom, enjoy each other, share this fantastic feast, and get ready for some spectacular fireworks over the lake when the sun goes down."

"Here, here," Owen shouted out, raising his drink.

"Here, here," Jon and Andrew echoed, raising their bottles along with the others.

Marcus stood with Anna on his left and Jeannie on his right. Caught up in the moment, Marcus reached his left arm around Anna's waist to pull her closer, but she tensed slightly—enough that Marcus got the message and relaxed his embrace. Puzzled, Marcus glanced down at Anna. She glanced back up at him with a closed-lip smile that showed a veiled self-conscious edginess. Marcus returned a smile, then, they both looked away. At the same time, Marcus felt a slight brush against his right hand, which dangled freely. He turned slightly to where Jeannie stood brushing her left arm against his right. She looked straight ahead with a confident grin. Then, crossed her arms and looked up at Marcus, as if she sensed his glance, and smiled.

"Dive in, everyone," Lauren invited. The entire moment spanned fewer than ten seconds, and Marcus knew he would not soon forget what it felt like to stand between Jeannie's warmth and Anna's unexpected coolness.

8. Getting personal

Marcus felt a cheerful lightness this July the fifth morning, sitting on the bench next to the lake trail near the water's edge of the Holman property. In about fifteen minutes Jeannie would come down the trail to his right.

Having the family together last night might have been my best night in years, Marcus thought. Anna was charming, of course. Yet, she seemed to act more like a well-behaved guest than one of the family. I felt like she was genuinely happy to be here, but she wasn't quite all here. Then, there was that unexplainable tension in her. Wha was with that stiffening up when I put my arm around her before dinner? And she left as soon as the fireworks were over, claiming a long day with the parade and all, and having to get an early start this morning to catch up at work. I expected her to linger awhile so we could have some private time, but, oh well, we live busy lives, I guess. I'll be glad when this campaign is over and we can get back to a more normal pace—whatever that is.

Jeannie, on the other hand, acted as if she belonged and was completely at ease with one and all. But, after all, she had been staying with Andy and Susie regularly so Lauren and Jarod could enjoy more date nights. Lauren says Jeannie eagerly accepts any invitation to come over and even changes plans to accommodate them.

I don't quite get Anna. Maybe I went a little overboard, hugging Anna so tightly when I saw her. I was so excited she was here as my girlfriend for a family event. And she was attentive, but not overly affectionate the rest of the evening, like she was afraid I was going to lay some PDA on her in front of everyone. Jeannie, on the other hand, Jeez, every time I turned around she was right there. She wasn't grabby or anything, but she would brush my arm or just stand as close as she could.

Maybe I should ask her about it this morning? Maybe not. I don't want to embarrass her. Maybe I'm reading too much into it.

She did get my attention, though. The way she was dressed. She wore more makeup than I usually see on her. Like she was making an effort. Come on, Marcus, she's a kid. Nothing there. Just a friend.

No doubt there have been some changes since last year at this time. I was about three months into my promotion, and I thought I was doing fine. I didn't have a love life of any kind and no prospects. Just too focused on my work.

Now look at me. Some of the changes were brutal. That week in October when Erin lowered the boom on me about my job performance. I was so angry, and disappointed, and embarrassed. But, hey, I came out OK. Had to suck up my pride and learn to take advice–a moment of truth for me. I didn't realize I was so full of myself. Elliot was a godsend as a mentor. Whenever I get a little off balance, he's been there to prop me up and set me straight. Plus, he's just such a cool dude. I believe I've turned the corner with my team. They seem closer as a unit, and I'm relying on them more to work that way since I've been pulled into this leadership development project with HR.

Theresa, too. I see her almost every day at work. "Wingman," she called herself at Lizzie's. She is always near. And my number one fan at work. She said she wanted to make me a legend, and I'm beginning to think she's working overtime on it. I know she wants more of a relationship with me. But give her credit, she's kept her word about boundaries, respecting my relationship with Anna and all. If I weren't with Anna, would I have already brought Theresa home to meet my family? An interesting thought, Marcus, an interesting thought. Isn't it interesting how I've kept Theresa at arm's length, and yet, I let Desiree penetrate my defenses? That was a hell of a night, Marcus. One you won't soon forget. I wonder how she's doing? Maybe I should ask Jim Bob about her? Naw, let well enough alone. What does that say about my openness to change?

"I do declare,' Marcus Winn, "you are easy to sneak up on when you are deep in thought," Jeannie was in the coy southern belle voice again.

"I guess I do zone out here," Marcus chuckled. "But, hey, look at you!" Marcus stood, and as he did, Jeannie embraced him snuggly. Marcus hugged her in return. *Let's keep this brotherly,* he thought, trying to find that balance between affectionate and intimate. He stepped back, *Wow, she looks gorgeous this morning. Like she suddenly blossomed into a woman and I'm just really noticing her for the first time. Maybe it's just my imagination, but I wonder if she's trying to get my attention? She's only eighteen, Marcus. Keep a lid on it.*

Jeannie started strolling down the trail. Marcus fell in beside her.

"Can we take our time today and not jog like we usually do? I have a lot to talk about, and I want you to myself for as long as I can have you." Jeannie looked at Marcus hopefully.

"Sure, just hanging around the house today. Emily, Owen, Mom and Dad stayed over."

"I love being with your family. I've never known a family that shows their love for each other so freely. I didn't know that even existed," Jeannie said.

"I know we're all glad you came our way." Marcus changed the subject, "So, everything seems to be settling down for you. Moving in with Christine and all."

"I was surprised how at home I felt there so quickly. After her husband was killed in Afghanistan, she didn't want to be alone. Lucky for me that Anna knew about her and introduced us. We talk a lot at night, and I think that helps her."

"How long were they together?"

"Over ten years. Tim died in a helicopter crash a little over a year ago."

"Kids?"

"A boy. Tyler. He's five now."

"That must be an adjustment for him. Losing his dad and all."

"More for Christine. Tyler was so young when it happened. Christine's problem is trying to keep Tim's memory alive for Tyler."

"How's that going?"

"She tells him stories about his dad and shows him pictures in a memory book she made. It seems to help Christine more than Tyler. I kind of know what it's like to lose a dad, you know?"

"You haven't talked about that much. Only what you told me about him moving to Chicago after the divorce. I'm glad I got to meet him at your graduation."

"Dad and I were close. I didn't understand why I had to stay with my mom. That decision was made for me. I'm determined to be in control of my own life from now on. One thing for sure, Marcus," Jeannie's expression hardened, "I'm never going to rely on a man to take care of me."

"I have no doubt that you'll be able to take care of yourself."

Jeannie stopped and turned to Marcus, looking him directly in the eyes, "Men just have it so much easier. Most men still treat women like objects. You ask a guy why he was first attracted to his wife or girlfriend, and I guarantee you the first words out of his mouth are, 'she's so pretty.' Disgusting." Jeannie started up the path again, picking up her pace slightly. Marcus matched her.

"I would agree somewhat, but I think a lot of guys are attracted to other things."

"What about you? What attracted you to Anna? You can't tell me that looks weren't part of it?"

Marcus felt like he needed to make the counterpoint, "Well, when I first saw Anna, she was in jeans, a team t-shirt, wearing a ball cap with her pony tail sticking out the back. If she had make up on, it wasn't much. But what I noticed first was how focused she was on coaching Andy's soccer team. She just drew me in, you know, as a spectator, to the flow of the match. Those little boys were the only thing on her mind. But then, after the match, I did notice how lovely she is."

"You can say it, Marcus. She has a great bod," Jeannie emphasized the point.

"Admittedly, but my point is that wasn't the first thing I noticed about her."

"Anyway. My mom relied on her looks to catch a man. I know how much time she puts into keeping fit and staying pretty for Nick, like it's the only thing he cares about. Honestly, I don't know what he cares about. But he seems to be totally into Mom, so I guess it works for them. I just won't be a trophy wife. The last thing I want is to feel like I have to be picked by a man who can take care of me. I'll do the picking, thank you."

"I have no doubt," Marcus did not elaborate.

"Obviously, Anna's a beautiful woman. And smart. And successful. She'd be tough competition for any woman. I see why you like her so much," Jeannie admitted.

"There's more to it," Marcus added. "I mean, there's gotta be sparks, too. You know, that romantic connection, that feeling you get when you're together."

"And I suppose Anna does that for you?" Jeannie queried.

Marcus hesitated, "Yeah."

Jeannie stopped abruptly causing Marcus to stop and turn back toward her standing in the middle of the trail, "Marcus, you don't sound very convincing to me. What's the deal? Everyone thinks you two are a hot item, a sure thing."

"I haven't told them any different," Marcus went on.

Jeannie interrupted, "But?"

"But . . ." Marcus paused unsure whether to continue this line of discussion, then continued, "But . . . Anna and I are still deciding just how serious we want to get. There's a lot changing in both of our lives right now. We haven't been able to spend as much time together as I expected, the work and all," Marcus could not believe he was confessing this to Jeannie.

Jeannie pressed, "So you all aren't . . . I mean, you haven't . . ."

Marcus cut her off, anticipating her meaning, "No." He hesitated. "No. I mean, she was raised a devout Catholic, and she has some definite ideas, you know, about stuff like that, and—"

"And so you haven't had sex yet? After how many months?" Jeannie asked incredulously.

"And so, what's wrong with that?" Marcus retorted.

Jeannie broke out in a wide smile, folding her arms and rocking back on one leg, "Nothing. Absolutely nothing."

"I don't know how we got off on this, but you're the only one I've had this conversation with. I'd appreciate it if you keep this between us. It will eventually work out one way or another," Marcus said almost pleading, while a spontaneous flashback to Williston and Desiree hit unexpectedly, *"If she isn't lovin' you every chance she gets by now, she's a fool."*

"Oh, don't worry about that. I won't breathe a word," Jeannie promised.

Marcus started walking again, and Jeannie paced him, "Let's change the subject and talk about you for a while. You said you had a lot to discuss," Marcus said. "What about you? I never hear you talk about any boys. Is there anyone you are interested in?"

"There's no one at school, and I don't get around that much," Jeannie admitted.

"I would think boys would be trying to get your attention."

"We're back to that looks thing again, Marcus. The boys check me out because of my looks. I know because none of them have actually tried to get to know me. I can see it in their eyes, and that turns me totally off," Jeannie said disgustingly.

"But yesterday," Marcus caught himself.

"Yesterday, what?" Jeannie stopped and stared into Marcus's eyes.

"Yesterday," Marcus chose his words carefully, "yesterday, the way you were dressed. It wasn't like anything I've seen you wear before."

"Well, you've only seen me dancing or jogging with you. I'm hot, Marcus. I'm a pretty woman when I fix up. I wanted everyone to see me as a young woman, not as a kid–the babysitter. I deserve to be at the adult table. There are countries, you know, where I would already be married off by now and have babies," Jeannie protested with a certain tone of indignation.

"Point taken," Marcus conceded. "You definitely have my attention as a young woman, and I won't ever think of you as a kid again. Trust me." Marcus paused and smiled down into Jeannie's searching expression. "I was just curious," Marcus backed off and changed course, "So what other Jeannie news do you have for me?"

Jeannie paused, relaxing her defensive posture and became suddenly excited, "My big news. The big news is I'm starting a business through the dance studio," Jeannie flashed a huge smile.

"That sounds exciting. How'd this come about?"

"Well, Ms. Rippetoe, the studio owner, you know, suggested we partner on it since I'm interested in photography, and I had shown her some of the photos I've been taking."

"She's an entrepreneur herself," Marcus added.

"Tell me. Anyway, she said she would make me the exclusive photographer for the studio in exchange for 25 percent of net profits. She would promote the service. She will pay for a website. I will photograph the girls individually and in dance teams and shoot candids at recitals. We sell prints with the Rippetoe Studio logo and my own personal brand stamped on the photos. I will still teach. She thinks I can make more money beyond what she can pay me as a teacher. Maybe double what I earn now."

"Sounds like a great opportunity . . . for both of you. A partnership," Marcus encouraged.

"And you made it possible with that camera as a graduation gift," Jeannie leapt into an exuberant embrace around Marcus's waist. Marcus hugged her around the shoulders and squeezed her snuggly, briefly, then released and took a step back, mindful of his earlier thoughts to keep it brotherly.

"I'm proud of you, Jeannie. You never cease to amaze me," Marcus became conscious that he was still holding her hands, and gently, slowly released his grip.

"Not just another pretty face, huh?" Jeannie smiled, blinking rapidly in a flirty way.

"Ms. Rippetoe obviously sees something in you to bring you into her studio as a teacher, and now as a business partner. I guess this means you'll be hanging around Springfield for the foreseeable future?" Marcus said continuing the walk.

"I'm not in as big of a hurry to get out of town as I was last year," Jeannie admitted. "After all, you still come up here all the time, and I like having you close. I feel safe with you. I feel like if I really needed you for some reason, you'd be here in a flash. Who knows what changes we have in store? Right?"

"Absolutely, Jeannie, absolutely. Anything is possible," and Marcus felt Jeannie take his hand in hers.

"I feel that way, too." Jeannie agreed.

They walked in silence along the lake path, everything being said that needed to be said for that moment.

They came to one of the benches along the trail. Marcus led Jeannie toward it, "Let's stop for a minute." They sat, allowing Marcus to release Jeannie's hand naturally.

They sat quietly looking out over the still lake.

Jeannie spoke first, "What else is going on, Marcus? I only get snapshots of what's happening in your life. Things that come up in messages and stuff Lauren says about you from time to time. And I never get to talk to you about your day. And I'm envious of Anna, who gets to talk to you every day probably, and that she knows everything about you, and I'm left just . . . just . . . I don't know," her voice trailed off, "I'm sounding like a silly little girl now," Jeannie stopped.

"You know that sketch you made of me in Andy's sketchbook the first time you came over to Lauren's? Lauren framed it and gave it to me. I have it on the end table next to my sofa at home."

"That was just a spur of the moment thing," Jeannie said shyly.

"Lauren said you captured that expression like I was searching for something. Every time I glance at that sketch I ask myself what I'm looking for. We've talked about this before, you know. I get to thinking how much has changed in such a short time—"

"Tell me about it," Jeannie interjected.

"Change comes at you from all sides, and it doesn't ask you if it's OK or if you're ready for it. It's relentless. About when you think you have things back under control, something else hits you. I remember you told me when we first met that we're all just trying to get by, to figure out life as we go, and that's so true. Even when we make plans and do our best to lay out our way, life happens, and it hasn't read our script about how things are supposed to go."

"Tell me about it," Jeannie repeated, stretching her legs straight and pointing her toes. Marcus noticed her

> ## *"Change comes at you from all sides, and it doesn't ask you if it's OK or if you're ready for it."*

muscular quadriceps through the gray and orange compression shorts. She yawned involuntarily, releasing the tension in her chest with a deep exhale.

"That day I met you I was afraid I might lose my job. I got blindsided the day before, and I had to face up to the ugly truth about how I had been doing, or not doing, my job as a team leader. That was hard until I got it in my head that I needed to change. Once I got more on the right track, another series of changes happened that have worked out pretty well. You and Anna have been a big part of those good changes."

"Good things," Jeannie agreed. "I was having a bad day, too, if you recall."

"Yeah, so I found out," Marcus agreed.

"All I knew was that my so-called life sucked at that moment. I wanted out, but the only way out I could think of was to use my looks to get what I wanted. You made me see and believe that I could be more than that. Now, I know I can, and that's a good thing," Jeannie's tone perked up.

"Yes, a good thing," Marcus echoed, "And look at

what's happened to me since then. It led to me being asked to make that presentation at the leadership retreat."

"You were awesome. I was so proud of you," Jeannie looked up at Marcus smiling and laid her hand on his thigh.

"All I could think about that afternoon was how I wanted to tell Anna all about it."

"Oh," Jeannie glanced toward her lap, sounding disappointed. She slid her hand from Marcus's thigh and folded her arms.

"But Anna's life was changing, too, and she wasn't available." Marcus sensed the change in Jeannie's voice, "But you, Jeannie. You were the next person who came to mind that I wanted to share that moment with, because I so wanted to share it with someone I cared for, and who I knew cared for me. Remember how we walked around this lake together a few days before that speech? You gave me so much to think about. You helped me know what to say."

Jeannie pointed her toes and kicked her legs, stretching them out, "I remember dancing with you at the labyrinth," Jeannie recalled.

"Yeah, so do I. And that analogy of leading and dancing made so much sense—about boundaries, and leaders taking the first step, and everything," Marcus paused. Jeannie gazed out over the lake. Marcus continued in a more reflective tone, "My life changed during that speech, Jeannie. What you couldn't see on the video was how awesome I felt about myself. I had a room full of executives in the palm of my hand. Successful, powerful leaders listening to me. What a rush . . . what a rush."

Jeannie rubbed the tops of her legs with her palms

and kneaded them simultaneously with her thumbs and fingers. "I guess we've all changed a lot lately. I know how wrapped up Anna is in the campaign. I've only talked to her a couple of times since she got so involved, but I know she's really excited about the important people she's met and the big law firm she's working with from Atlanta."

"Yeah, we've talked about that, on the few occasions I get to talk to her myself, usually late at night. Sometimes I fall asleep on my sofa waiting for her to call," Marcus confessed.

"Well, not all change is what we hoped for, I guess," Jeannie mused.

"Anyway, I'll see her Saturday morning at Greer's rally. She's eager for me to meet him. Supposedly, she's scheduled some one-on-one time with him before the event. For a while, I thought she had something going with him, but she told me there was nothing like that, and that I would like him, so I guess I'll find out Saturday."

"Are you jealous?" Jeannie asked.

"No, not jealous," Marcus was quick to respond. "When I first started seeing Anna, I could picture her as part of my family, as that one someone I've been looking for. She has it all—all those things you said about her earlier, and yes, beautiful, too," Marcus dropped his gaze to his lap. He noticed he was wringing his hands slowly. "Now, I'm not sure."

"The election will be over in November. Things will probably get back to normal then," Jeannie said.

"In the meantime, Jeannie Irwin," Marcus pivoted, "you have a business to build and a whole new life to get on with. You've got a lot of changes in store for you, and you can count on me to be right there with you to cheer you on."

"One thing that will never change, Marcus, is how important you are to me. I want you in my life forever," Jeannie returned her hand to the top of Marcus's leg.

"You can count on it," Marcus laid his hand on the top of Jeannie's and squeezed it briefly.

"Hey, I feel like jogging a little now. You up to it?" Jeannie suggested.

"You bet," Marcus agreed, "enough of this serious life talk for one morning."

"Lauren will think I've kidnapped you if you're not back soon. And I have to do some stuff with Christine this afternoon anyway," Jeannie said.

* * *

Marcus entered the dining room off the veranda. Emily, Owen, Lauren, and his mother, Melanie, sat around the table sipping coffee, a familiar scene when all were together.

"Enjoy your walk with Jeannie?" Lauren asked.

Marcus was already filling the kettle to heat water. "We had a really good talk. More leisurely this time," Marcus nodded going about his chore.

"I heard you go out the door about eight his morning, and it's eleven now. Must have had a lot to talk about," Lauren sipped her coffee looking over the cup's brim expectedly at Marcus.

"Actually, we did. I learned Ms. Rippetoe is fronting Jeannie in a new business venture taking pictures of the studio's students and documenting recitals and competitions. I think it could really take off for her," Marcus said.

Melanie added, "That Jeannie is a doll," she said looking around the table. "She impresses me every time we talk. She comes across a lot older than eighteen."

"No kidding," Owen saw an opening, "I mean, she could easily pass for twenty-two, twenty-three maybe. She just has that mature way about her, not like you'd expect from a kid."

"And she's a knockout," Emily finished where she knew Owen wanted to go, but wouldn't quite say it. Everyone nodded, saying, "Yes, um-hum, yeah," almost in choir-like unison.

Marcus headed them off, "All right everyone, I know where you're going with this, and you're on the wrong track, so just get off it. Besides, she's just a kid, eighteen. I'm twenty-eight."

"I remember when I was eighteen," Melanie rolled her eyes, grinning like she was playing an old scene in her mind. "I was hot, and hot, if you know what I mean."

"Mom," Emily cut her off, "we don't need to know everything."

"Well, we all saw how she was dressed yesterday, and it wasn't for any of our benefit," Melanie paused, and no one spoke. She continued, "Don't get me wrong, she wasn't inappropriate, and I'm not bashing her at all. It's just obvious to me that she has a major crush on you, Marcus, to say the least."

The kettle whistled, as if on cue.

"Mom, I just spent nearly three hours with her, and she never said or did anything inappropriate, or came on to me, or anything like that," Marcus defended.

"Jeannie is too classy to be so forward. I can tell," Melanie said. "But she knew exactly what she was doing. She knew Anna would be here with you, and that you would be ga-ga over Anna all the time, which you were. She just wanted you to notice her, and anyway, how do you compete with Anna?"

"Jeannie did say that all she wanted was for everyone to see her as an adult," Marcus defended.

Lauren explained, "I dearly love Jeannie, and she talks about you all the time, wants to know what you are doing, how you are doing, when you are coming up next. She beams when we talk about you."

"She does text me about once a week, wanting to know when I'm coming up again, but that's about all the contact we have," Marcus said.

"Believe me, she would talk to you every day if she could, Marcus," Lauren said. "We just thought you should be more aware of what we see, so you won't hurt her feelings unintentionally."

"And the age thing," Emily jumped in, "remember, Owen is twelve years older than me. He was too busy being a doctor to fall in love. And then he met me and that was that."

"And that was that," Owen echoed, "we never thought twice about age."

"Jeannie has several years of finding herself in front of her, and I'm not going to complicate things for her, or for myself, by getting involved like that," Marcus deflected.

"I'm sure you're right about that," Lauren said, "and I know you are still locked in on Anna. Just be aware of Jeannie's feelings, and be wise about how you treat her. And if it ever turns out that Jeannie is the one for you, we would understand why."

"OK. Message received. And thanks for caring," Marcus took the last sip of his tea and sat the cup in the sink.

"What are your plans for tonight?" Lauren asked.

"Hang around here to be with my big sisters, I guess.

As long as Anna is doing double duty at the firm and on Greer's campaign, that doesn't leave much time for me. I'll see her for breakfast tomorrow, then we are going to Greer's rally."

"Well, it's family night at the Holman's since everyone's here. Susie has ordered up an UNO smack down," Lauren said.

"I'm ready for it," Marcus laughed.

"Bring it on," Owen answered the challenge.

* * *

That feeling of disequilibrium washed over Marcus as he lay in bed on top of the covers. *I don't know what to think about everyone's comments and observations about Jeannie. I really don't want to lead her on, and I really don't think it's smart getting mixed up with a teenager. Anna told me about an obsessive relationship she experienced in college and how that went bad. I don't want to stumble into anything like that. Especially now.*

Am I kidding myself about Anna? Is she really not into me, and I can't see it, and she won't say it either? She's had the chance to pull the plug on our relationship, such as it is, and she hasn't. I take her at her word that she wants to play this out.

Are my expectations about Anna unrealistic? I've built up in my mind that we could be a great couple, but then, what changes would we both have to make for that to happen? Obviously, we would have to live in the same city, get married eventually. It's more realistic to me that she could move to Tulsa and work for a firm there. I'm sure there are several firms that would welcome her. I obviously have to stay in Tulsa as things stand now. It seems that she has more flexibility to move than I do.

What about Theresa? Theresa makes no bones about wanting a relationship with me. She would be a lot better fit since she's already in Tulsa, and we have a lot in common professionally. I know I'm very comfortable being with her, although we've not dated to get to know each other that way. I know there's an infatuation there–both ways–but is that enough for the makings of a deeper relationship between us? So many changes. Which way to go?

Look at the changes I've already had to deal with.

My job being on the line. That was a brutal truth kind of change. A lot of friction. And Jim Bob. That began with a lot of friction, the way he insulted me with the first words out of his mouth. He is change resistant about oil and gas. He's dead set that alternative energy is a fad, and what difference does it make anyway in our lifetime? He has absolutely no scope, no reference, other than the here and now. But come to find out, there's a whole different side of Jim Bob that's actually pretty likable once you get past that hard shell he projects. Just have to understand where he's coming from. Glad I took time to get to know him.

The other changes for me have evolved one step at a time. One situation leads to the next, and the next in kind of a natural order of things. Even my team has evolved as a unit as we went through the challenges we've faced and overcome since I became the team leader. I see each of the team members growing, except for Brad.

Johnstone Energy is in a transition that began before I arrived. Nelson's fascination with renewable energy is changing the mix of his business. He's trying to blend renewable with the traditional fossil fuel business, and right now it's more like mixing oil and water. Not sure it's going to happen. But the entire energy sector is in transi-

tion with the complications of global energy. That's why Congressman Wakefield wants to talk with me, I guess.

Marcus felt sleep overtaking him as his mind drifted. *All I really want is a place like this.* He looked to his right as he lay quietly. *Who would occupy that place in my bed? Anna? That's looking more remote day by day. Theresa? I could definitely imagine that. Jeannie? Hmmmmmm.* Marcus drifted off, smiling.

9. Leaders lead

Anna was waiting for Marcus just outside the entry to a private dining room at the Corner Café where Eric Greer's campaign team would meet for morning assignments leading up to the 10:00 a.m. rally. The thick, sweet aroma of the café's locally famous cinnamon rolls mingling with the competing fragrances of flavored coffee overwhelmed Marcus.

Marcus approached Anna, reached out, hugged her around her shoulders, and kissed her on the left cheek, "Morning, sweetheart." he whispered in her ear.

"Marcus," Anna protested in a whisper pushing back slightly, "we're in public."

"All the same, I'm glad to see you," Marcus smiled, looking her in the eyes. "Are we the first ones here?"

Anna glanced down self-consciously, half turning toward the door, "No, a few of the staff are inside already. They went through the buffet. Are you hungry?"

"Not really. I think I'll just have something to drink for now."

"Eric should be here soon. He's looking forward to meeting you," Anna said more relaxed.

"Did you got caught up at work?" Marcus inquired.

Anna sighed deeply, "Finally," She said exhaling. "This case I'm working on is running me ragged. It's complex."

"And then there's the campaign on top of that," Marcus probed.

"Even much of that has taken a back seat to work recently," Anna explained. "I haven't seen anyone with the campaign since the parade. They must think I've abandoned them."

"I thought you were just handling the local legal aspects," Marcus continued.

"It started out that way, but Eric likes having me as part of his core crew, and I enjoy the energy of the campaign. I'm learning so much about the behind the scenes of campaigning. Will you be able to stay through the rally?"

"Yes. I want to see what all you do, and I want to see what a congressional candidate does to win votes," Marcus affirmed.

"That's the spirit," Anna glowed. "Oh, here's Eric now," Anna stood up taller, looking past Marcus into the crowded café dining area.

Eric made his way between the tables, stopping to shake hands and introducing himself as he went. Several patrons knew him and called him by name as he passed, offering their support and encouragement.

Greer was dressed in starched jeans with a pressed crease and a heavily starched blue and white striped oxford shirt with a "Go With Greer" logo monogrammed above the pocket. His sleeves were neatly rolled up to give the impression of casualness and approachability. His stout, hairy forearms suggested strength. He wore Cole Haan loafers. Nothing ostentatious, except the Rolex. Greer was slightly shorter than Marcus, maybe five-eleven. His belly hinted of a paunch. His short curly dark brown hair was a bit mussed, making a part unnecessary. Marcus noticed several shallow pockmarks on his cheeks, suggesting a battle with adolescent acne.

His well tanned face was clean shaven but looked like he could sport an impressive beard if he chose. He came across very middleclass, although Marcus knew he was a multi-millionaire commercial real estate developer.

Marcus was glad he decided to clean up for the occasion with dress slacks, a starched long sleeve gray and white checked shirt and polished Jack Erwin loafers. The thought flashed, *Am I pulling a Jeannie?* referring to his sudden instinct to compare his appearance to Greer's, like male birds-of-paradise seeking to impress the female.

Anna provided introductions, "Eric, I'd like to present my friend, Marcus Winn. Marcus, this is Eric Greer."

Greer extended his hand, looking Marcus in the eyes with a toothy smile, "Marcus, it's a pleasure to meet you. I'm glad you could join us today. Anna has told me about you."

"My pleasure, also. Glad it worked out. I've been curious to finally see what's got Anna so excited about politics," Marcus returned.

"Well, you'll get a dose of it today. Are you hungry? I'm going to go through the buffet right quick," Eric suggested.

Anna jumped in, "I'll have Carrie get that for you, Eric, so you and Marcus can talk. She knows what you like. OK?"

"Sure, thanks," Eric replied a little surprised at Anna's offer. He motioned Marcus toward the private dining room, "Let's make ourselves comfortable. I want to hear about your work in renewable energy."

"Marcus, I'll get your tea. Are you sure you don't want anything?" Anna offered.

"Since you asked, how about some fruit and a side of bacon?" Marcus answered.

"OK. Be right back," Anna turned to the buffet area.

Eric led Marcus to a table opposite where the others sat so they could have more privacy. "We're lucky Anna's firm assigned her to the campaign. We have a high-powered PR firm out of Atlanta that does most of our work. They do the heavy lifting legally, but I wanted local talent on the team. Anna did a marvelous job for a lawsuit I was fending off. She's smart, poised, professional, and hungry to learn, and I believe keeping that local involvement in the campaign is important to my credibility."

"She puts everything into her work, for sure," Marcus agreed.

"How long have you worked for Johnstone Enterprises?"

"Almost six years."

"What's it like to work for a renewable energy firm that's part of a huge oil and gas company?" Eric asked.

"I get that question a lot, " Marcus began. "The oil and gas side is pretty traditional. Some think Mr. Johnstone is a bit eccentric to venture out into renewable, but I think he knows exactly what he's doing and why."

"Do you ever worry Millennium might get lopped off, or sold?"

"Not as long as Mr. Johnstone retains control. I know he is committed to support renewable as part of the larger energy production sector," Marcus assured.

"What do you think are the biggest hurdles wind energy has to overcome to be profitable?" Eric asked.

"It's not like hydro or coal, or even nuclear, because you can turn all those on and off as you need production. With wind, you only get it when wind blows. That means storage is key, and we don't have storage figured out," Marcus answered.

"What part of the system does your team work on?" Eric asked.

"We're on the generation side. Our task is to improve the efficiency of our turbines."

" How is progress on that?"

"We had some big improvements last year. I can't go into that because it's proprietary," Marcus answered.

"How about now?" Eric probed.

"We've been going back through all our technology to find better ways and better materials. It's like losing weight. You make a lot of progress early because you have a long way to go. It's the last few pounds that are the hardest. Our efficiencies went up dramatically early. Now we are eeking out the last efficiencies we can find. Even at that, we're pretty damn efficient as it is," Marcus said proudly.

"Sounds like distribution might be where the gains can come," Eric summarized.

"If we can get production closer to the end user that will help. But right now the wind fields are in rural areas and no one wants windmills in their back yard or in urban areas," Marcus confessed.

"Renewable energy is a major part of my agenda, Marcus. Collins, the incumbent, is a climate change denier. I think he's vulnerable on this issue. I just need a good way to tell this story so everyone can see themselves benefiting directly from it. I'd be open to hearing some of your ideas," Eric invited.

"Sure. I'll give it some thought," Marcus agreed.

Anna and Carrie returned together with food and drinks. Anna took a seat at the table. Carrie returned to her tasks with the other crew members.

Eric sipped his coffee and continued, "I was telling

---

3 Roles in the change dynamic.

Sponsors of change: *those who, by virtue of their position, can authorize change.*

Advocates of change:
those who see the need for change and seek to convince and persuade sponsors to authorize the change.

Instruments of change:
those who must comply with the changed state, or live by the rules the sponsors have set in place.

Marcus that renewable energy is a major part of our story."

"May I ask a personal question?" Marcus asked.

"Sure."

"You're a successful businessman, why do you want to be a congressman?"

"Simple. I want to make change happen, and change only happens when the sponsors of change say so," Eric said matter-of-factly and took another sip from the café ceramic mug.

"Sponsors? What do you mean?" Marcus asked.

"In any organization there are one or more people who, by virtue of their position, have the power to say what the rules will be for the organization. They are the sponsors. Institutional change happens only when they say so," Eric explained.

"But as a successful businessman, don't you have a lot of influence?"

"In my business, as CEO, I can sponsor change just like Nelson Johnstone does for his company. But as a citizen, all I can do is advocate change, unless I'm one of the sponsors. Here in Springfield it's the city council. At the state level it's the state legislature. At the national level it's the U.S. Congress–senators and representatives. I think my best bet to make changes that I believe are important is being in the House of Representatives," Eric paused to take a bite of his scrambled eggs.

"And what do you feel so strongly about that you want to change it?" Marcus probed.

Eric began his answer while still chewing a piece of toast, "Education, economic opportunity, and equality."

"And how does energy fit into those?" Marcus asked curiously.

"It's impacted by two of those three directly. Economic opportunity is obvious because of the jobs the renewable energy field will continue to create and support. Education is crucial because we need the engineers and technicians to support the full range of the industry. We must have educated, creative, and skilled workers, or we can't have the economic opportunity we want. Everything is interrelated."

"And how do you get that message to take hold?"

"Storytelling." Eric said emphatically

"Storytelling?" Marcus repeated for clarity.

"Yep. Storytelling. Stay for the rally, and you'll see what I mean," Eric dabbed the corners of his mouth with a napkin.

"This is my first political rally," Marcus confessed.

"But not your first rally," Eric interjected.

"What do you mean?"

"That company leadership retreat where you spoke, or church, for that matter. Those are rallies. Even the

"People want to be persuaded. They want to hear a clear story that they can relate to. They want to see themselves in the story, and they want to feel they are going to be safe and happy."

Bible says to meet together and stir one another up to do good. That's all a rally is. People of like mind meeting together to stir each other up," Eric took the last bite of his toast and refilled his coffee from the carafe.

"I guess I never thought of it that way," Marcus admitted.

"People want to be persuaded. They want to hear a clear story that they can relate to. They want to see themselves in the story, and they want to feel they are going to be safe and happy. My job is to craft that story and tell it like I believe it with all my heart. Otherwise, why should they?"

"What about facts and data? Don't they matter?"

"Sure, the story must be solid on facts, and the story has to stay true to the facts. But if all you do is recite facts, people stop listening. Tell a story people can feel part of, and they will convince themselves that you are right."

Anna interjected, "Eric, tell Marcus what you told me when you saw the video of his speech."

"Yeah, Marcus, I thought you did a great job of storytelling. You really got everyone on your side because they could see themselves in those stories. And you project a solid, charismatic presence on stage. I encourage you to develop your speaking talent. It is a gift to be able to relate to large audiences like you are talking to each of them individually," Eric praised.

"Thank you. I appreciate the compliment," Marcus replied then continued, "But what about those politicians who talk only about being afraid or of losing our way of life? Why are they so popular?"

"One word. Change. It's all about change, or more specifically, the fear of change. We know from research that people are more afraid of losing something than they are hopeful of gaining something. We are risk averse. We will fight to protect what we have. In that sense, we don't want to change because we can't get a clear vision of what better looks lile, and if it can happen for us. We want guarantees. But in life, there simply are no guarantees," Eric explained.

"I can identify with that," Marcus admitted. .

"Me, too," Anna agreed.

Marcus asked, "How do you balance those?"

"That's tricky," Eric admitted. "First of all you have to paint a clear and vivid picture of where you want to go. That's where I think most politicians fall short. Then, you have to show everyone how they can get there with minimum, or no risk."

"Why do you think politicians fall short on that?" Marcus had to know.

"Because they don't know. They don't know where they are going," Eric was adamant.

Marcus waited in silence.

Eric continued, "Here's what happens. We spend a lot of time talking about what we don't want. We don't want waste in our business. We don't want corrupt politicians. We don't want to get sick. We don't want others taking our jobs away from us or threatening our way of life. But not getting what you don't want, will never guarantee that you will get what you do want."

"Wait," Marcus perked up, "I've heard that exact same thing before, but from a teenager." Marcus turned to Anna, "Jeannie told me those exact same words a couple of months ago."

"Well, she's very wise about that. Take her advice," Eric emphasized.

Marcus continued, "I guess that's why politicians spend so much time going negative on the opponent or telling us we need to be afraid someone will steal our freedom."

Eric agreed, "You got it. Reason goes out the window when fear bangs on the door," Eric paused for a sip of water. "Marcus, there are three kinds of politicians. There are those who pander to the crowds. They shift their story to rev up whatever crowd they are in front of. The story changes from crowd to crowd, depending on their hot buttons. They take one position in front of one crowd and a slightly different one in front of another. Then, there's the puppet. The special interests that fund their campaign pull the strings. The problem is the audience thinks they are watching a real leader, when they are actually watching a wooden shell of the ultimate 'yes' man. Then there's the pathfinder. The visionary who can see the future, tell the story, and head out in that direction. The true believers will follow and bring others with them. Marcus, which of those are you?" Eric was looking Marcus straight into the eyes.

Marcus paused, glanced down into his empty cup, and looked back into Eric's expectant gaze, "I'd like to think I'm a pathfinder." Marcus replied.

"Reason goes out the window when fear bangs on the door."

"So would I, Marcus. So would I," Eric nodded as he spoke. "We tell people what they need to hear, not just what they want to hear. We share our passion and vision in our stories. We are change makers, Marcus. We show the way, because if we aren't causing positive change, we aren't leading."

Carrie walked up next to the table, "Eric, it's about time to go."

"OK, let's do this. Marcus, are you going over with us?"

"Yeah, sure. Anna gave me the directions."

"All right, then. And you'll get to meet my fiancé, Renee. She's handling all the advance publicity. I think we are doing a TV interview before the rally. I really enjoyed getting to meet you, Marcus. Remember to send me your ideas. Give them to Anna, and she'll pass them along. OK?"

"Sure thing," Marcus shook Eric's hand.

The entourage scampered out the door. Anna held back with Marcus.

"Do you see what I meant about Eric?" Anna took Marcus's hand.

"We are change makers. We show the way, because if we aren't causing positive change, we aren't leading."

"He seems sincere about what he's doing," Marcus said.

"And I think he can really make a difference. I want to help him win this election," Anna squeezed Marcus's hand.

"And you should. But where does that leave us? We barely have any contact now as it is. Am I losing you?" Marcus asked.

"Marcus, we had this talk recently. I don't know what to tell you today that would be any different. Let's just take this one step at a time. I'm just not moving at the same speed as you, but that doesn't mean I care any less. OK?"

"I understand," Marcus dropped Anna's hand.

Anna perked up, "Come on, we need to get over to the rally. You'll enjoy seeing Eric in front of an audience. He's a great communicator."

Marcus drove in silence to the college auditorium where Greer's rally was about to start. Anna would escort him backstage. *I know I've told Anna over and over about the kind of home and family I hope to have someday. She tells me that's a nice dream, but she never talks of herself as being part of that vision. Am I just talking to myself? I assumed she knew that she's the one my dream happens with–the woman of my dreams. I've been expecting Anna to be on the same path that I'm on, that we would find a way to be together. Maybe she's telling me that she sees a different future for herself.*

Think of Jeannie. She definitely sees her future and acts on it. Now, she's making it happen for herself. She's making the changes she needs to make to get what she wants.

What about my team at work? We seem to be stuck,

trying harder at the same thing to make our wind fields more productive. Do we need a different vision of what we are trying to accomplish? Do we need to blaze a new trail, find a new path forward?

What about how I see myself professionally? I can't say I have really envisioned my future with my company or my role in it. I've just let one thing lead to another. It's been positive, and I like the way it's going. What if I really thought through how it could be, how I want it to be? What changes would I have to make for that vision to come true? Who would be with me in that future?

Whitney Ellis is a change maker. She's one of those INPowered people I talked about in my leadership speech. She sees a need and acts on it to make things better—to lead change. Am I that kind of a change maker? Is this leadership class HR is developing an opportunity to make that change? What change do I believe in? What vision do I have for a different, better future? Is my influence limited to my team? My company? Johnstone Enterprises as a whole? The energy industry? Am I having another moment of truth?

Marcus steered his Z into the parking lot designated for the campus fine arts center. Dozens of people were entering the middle glass doors. A group wearing green t-shirts, advocating for environmental issues, passed out fliers. SUVs, pickups, and passenger cars filled the first five rows on either side of the central driveway. Looks like a big crowd. And it's still half-an-hour before time to start. Marcus circled around back to the first empty row and parked in the end space closest to the central drive.

Inside, a local rock band entertained early arrivers, covering classic hits. Some mingled in the aisles and in the foyer contributing to the buzz of anticipation. Vol-

unteers passed out "Go With Greer" placards to eager
supporters. True to her word, Anna, stood in front of
the stage waiting for him. She spotted him immediately
and waived enthusiastically for him to come down. "This
way," she said when Marcus reached the front, and she
hastened up the steps leading backstage. Marcus chased
behind.

Anna led Marcus to a dressing room. Two volunteers
controlling entry to the room recognized Anna and waived
her in. A group of eight supporters squeezed in, listening intently as a television reporter interviewed Greer in
a corner. Greer placards plastered the wall providing a
backdrop for maximum visual effect. Marcus recognized
Missouri's popular female U.S. Senator, Carol Manning,
standing near Greer. Marcus whispered in Anna's left
ear, "Now I'm impressed."

"It's exciting, isn't it," Anna replied, borderline giddy,
tilting her head slightly toward Marcus while her eyes
remained fixed on Greer.

Marcus could see it in Anna's unrestrained, exuberant energy, her smile, and the excitement in her eyes.
She's hooked, Marcus thought, sizing her up, zoned in on
Greer, hanging on his every word. *She is fully invested in
this campaign. It's obvious there's little or no room for me
in her world right now.*

Marcus felt his phone vibrate. He pulled it from his
pocked and glanced down holding it to his side. Jeannie.
"will I get to c u before u go back this p.m.? parade photos ready."

Marcus entered using only his left thumb, still holding the phone next to his leg, "ok where?"

"Christine's OK?"

"ok when done here."

"5733 Redhawk Ln"

"k" Marcus agreed, and retuned his phone to his pocket.

Marcus fought off the urge to excuse himself and leave early. Marcus looked down at Anna. She remained transfixed on Greer. *If I left, I wonder how long it would take her to notice?* He still wanted to see how Greer handled the crowd. Mostly, he wanted to hear Senator Manning speak before she introduced Greer. Marcus presumed that was her role today. The room was charged.

The TV camera's flood light went off, signaling the end of the interview. A hubbub swelled in the room. Greer's campaign manager whispered in his ear and escorted him toward the exit. The crowd parted to let Greer through. Greer stopped as he reached Marcus. He took Marcus's hand, pulled Marcus closer, and whispered in his ear, "Get clear about where you want to go, and go there, Marcus. Be that leader." And Greer skipped into the corridor and headed for the stage.

Anna grabbed Marcus's hand, "Come on," she urged and fell in line behind the entourage. By the time they reached the backstage area from which they would watch the rally, the emcee was announcing the first speaker. "And now ladies and gentlemen welcome Missouri's favorite U.S. Senator, the honorable Carol Manning." The

"Get clear about where you want to go, then go there."

crowd went wild to the band's arrangement of, Tom Petty's *Won't back down.*

* * *

Marcus walked briskly across the parking lot texting Jeannie as he went. "leaving rally. on my way over." *Hope it wasn't too obvious that I was ready to get out of there. Highlight was getting a photo with Senator Manning. Now there's a celebrity. Could be President. Got a totally different picture of Anna. Never seen here in her element before. Always had her on my turf and my terms. Guess we'll talk later. I just want to see what Jeannie's got going and get back home.*

"excited to c u. hurry. need directions?"

"got it on gps"

ok. I'll be ready."

Fifteen minutes later Marcus pulled up to 5733 Redhawk Lane, parked on the curb, hurried up the sidewalk, and rang the doorbell.

The door opened almost immediately as if Jeannie had been watching. Jeannie pulled the door wide open showing herself wearing a bikini with a sheer cover she left untied leaving the front open causing Marcus to freeze momentarily at first glance. Marcus had never seen that much of her exposed. Her red hair was pulled back in a bun like when she dressed to dance. She was barefoot and wore no makeup. Her emerald eyes sparkled. She was buff and absolutely breathtaking. *Damn, Jeannie, what's your game here? What do you have planned? I'm not sure I should touch you, and I'm pretty sure my eyes are popping out of my head.*

"Come in, Marcus. I'm so happy to see you. Welcome to my new home." Jeannie chirped as she took Marcus's hand and pulled him into the small foyer and closed the front door behind him. She reached to hug him, but Marcus only lightly patted her shoulder in acknowledgment, not sure exactly how to touch her, or where. "I hope you don't mind that I went ahead and dressed for the pool party I'm going to after you leave."

"Uh, no. Not at all," Marcus tried to sound natural. "Is Christine home? I was hoping to meet her," Marcus probed.

"Oh, she's already gone over to the party at one of her friend's. It came up all of a sudden, and she invited me along. Said you could come too, but I told her you were probably in a hurry to get back to Tulsa."

"Yeah, uh yeah, I can't stay long," Jeannie's out relieved Marcus.

"Too bad. I had such a good time with you the other day, and I hoped I would get to see you again. Anyway, I have everything set up here at the dining room table." Jeannie turned on her toes to show him the way.

Everything about her is hot and seductive. Marcus took a heavy breath and sighed. Jeannie heard him and looked over her shoulder.

"Are you OK? That was a big sigh."

"Yeah, fine." *Maybe the family was right about Jeannie. I need to be careful here. Marcus smiled reassuringly and followed Jeannie.* "This place is larger than it looks from the outside." Small talk seemed like a safe strategy.

"Yeah, I know. I was surprised too when I came over the first time," Jeannie replied. "My room is upstairs, and I have my own bathroom and everything. Lots of privacy. Would you like to see?"

Marcus cleared his throat, "No, uh, but thanks. I need to get on the road pretty quick." *Am I reading too much into all this? Better be careful.*

Jeannie had a laptop set up on the dining table. She pulled out the chair in front of it. "Sit here so I can sit beside you and show you through the gallery. Would you like something cold to drink?"

"No, I'm fine, thank you," Marcus cleared his throat.

"Are you sure you're OK? You seem nervous. I've never seen you like this before?" Jeannie stood beside her chair looking down into Marcus's eyes. Her bikini top was about eye level to him.

"No, uh," Marcus cleared his throat again, looking up into Jeannie's face, "I mean yeah. Yeah, I'm fine, except that I thought Christine would be here, and I feel a little awkward being alone with you in your house, and uh," Marcus cleared his throat again, "and you dressed like that."

Jeannie cackled spontaneously, "Surely you've been around women in bikinis before."

"Sure, but not you. I've never seen you dressed, if you want to call it that, dressed like this before." Marcus looked her up and down as he spoke.

Jeannie broke into her southern belle accent, "I do declare, Marcus. Do I cause you some fluster?" As she spoke, Jeannie fanned her face rapidly with her hand while batting her eyelashes.

"Come on. I'm not kidding, and don't tease me like that." Jeannie turned and walked into the kitchen as Marcus spoke. "In fact, you are flustering me right now. You're a beautiful girl–

"Woman!" Jeannie interrupted, retrieving a glass from the cabinet.

"Woman," Marcus corrected immediately, "and you said you wanted to be seen as a woman, and I definitely see that. There isn't much left to the imagination, and all these red-blooded American boy urges are running through me and I'm feeling a little confused right now."

Jeannie handed Marcus a glass of water, "You need this." She grinned as he took a sip.

"Well, I hadn't intended to make a point or cause you any discomfort by dressing this way, but I'm glad I did." Jeannie said as Marcus chugged the rest of the water. "Yes, Marcus, I am very comfortable in my body. I know I am attractive. And I'm starting to feel the things that I guess all women feel about themselves at my age." Jeannie sat next to Marcus facing him. "I know I want to be romanced and wooed, not jumped like a drunk prom date. Some day I will be . . . wooed, I mean. Who knows, it might be you . . . someday. But not today, not in the scrambled frame of mind you're in right now. And I've got way too much going on to get tangled up in a relationship right now. I'm starting a business and going to college and dancing and all. Marcus, I adore you," Jeannie put a hand on Marcus's right knee, then removed it when he tensed in reaction, "But my body is not what I want you to fall in love with. Someday you, or someone as equally awesome as you, will fall in love with a successful, confident, businesswoman and artist that I intend to be. So, relax," Jeannie took Marcus's hand and squeezed it, leaning in eye-to-eye, "I have no plans to jump your bones."

Jeannie released Marcus's hand and reached for the computer mouse. "Although, I'm sure it would be very enjoyable." The screen popped to life as Jeannie wiggled the mouse. "Now, let me show you some of my better images from the parade and some of the other things I've been working on."

Marcus spoke softly, "Thanks for clearing that up. I

was beginning to wonder if I had been leading you on unintentionally. The last thing I want to do is spoil what we have."

"Marcus, I've been soul searching since we met and since Anna started talking to me about her own life. I believe the right situation and the right guy will be there for me at the right time. Yeah, I've fantasized about being with you. I thought a couple of months ago that I wanted you to want me instead of Anna. Then it dawned on me that I was on the verge of following in my mother's footsteps, and that scared the crap out of me. I bet I've been back to the labyrinth a dozen times walking it and thinking about my life and who I am. I'm changing in so many ways, and my art helps me express it."

Marcus smiled and sighed, relieved. "You're amazing to me, Jeannie. You are wise beyond your years."

"Marcus, I believe there is a Divine energy that influences our lives. I think that energy caused you to find me on the trail that day. I think you needed me as much as I needed you, and we will always be part of each other, no matter what."

"No matter what, Jeannie. I promise," Marcus took Jeannie's left hand and raised it to his lips and kissed it without losing eye contact. "No matter what." He released her hand. "Now, show me what you've been working on."

10. Twilight

Marcus set the cruise control at exactly 75 miles per hour, and headed back down Interstate 44 to Tulsa. He did not trust his foot to keep the 370Z under 90, and the last thing he needed was to be pulled over by one of the state troopers who had shown up in force to patrol this holiday weekend. Marcus had been up and down this road more than a hundred times over the years; so, he let instincts take over the automatic routines of guiding the car to free his mind to make sense of the swirl of events and emotions that had swarmed him since Wednesday. The Marcus Winn who sped southwest on I-44 this Saturday afternoon was a different version of the Marcus Winn who had dashed expectantly eastbound up the highway Tuesday evening.

Why can't life be simpler? Why are there so many changes on so many fronts in my life right now? I thought I had everything under control in January. My promotion was secured, Anna had come into my life, and I thought I knew how the future was going to play out. At least I had made up my mind how I wanted it to play out.

Then, BOOM. Out of nowhere my team had to defend our project, which we did. I was riding high on that success only to find myself literally lost for words over the presentation I had agreed to give at the company's leadership retreat. Amy Capshaw pulled me out of that crisis, and I found a whole new side of myself I didn't know existed—motivational speaker. Who would have thought? Suddenly, I'm some kind of company celebrity, which I totally did not want for myself at all. It's to the point that people I never met, even a congressional candidate, have seen the video of the speech. And the company wants to build a leadership program out of my core ideas. Those are all good changes for me. I didn't set out to make them happen, but they did.

Even good changes can be totally disruptive. Like this perpetual road construction on the interstate. Marcus tapped the brakes to slow and merge into one lane where the interstate was being repaired. *I feel like my life is in a constant state of reconstruction. About the time I get up to speed and things seem to be in a flow, I have to hit the brakes and adjust. I know Monday I've got to walk into the lab and challenge my team to find ways to get a few more percentages of improvement in production efficiency from our wind field. Damn, when will it let up?*

And on top of that my love life is in a mess. Did I say "love life?" How can I call it a love life when I haven't had sex in . . . in . . . in, Jeez I can't call one night with Desiree a love life, as unbelievable as it was. As far as anything resembling a relationship? Tammy was the last one. She dumped me because I was a workaholic and didn't realize it, and now she's married with a new baby. So that makes it nearly three years ago. This is not normal, Marcus. Not normal. This has got to change.

Anna was going to be the one. She blew me away when we met, and for a while everything seemed to be going well. I could see a future with her, and I thought she was moving along in the same direction. Then, there was the Valentine Day melt down when I asked for an exclusive relationship, and yes, Marcus, that implied sleeping together. But Anna, as it turns out, was not on that page at all. "Let's wait until June," she said. But June came and went and we are farther from, not closer to that kind of a relationship. Now, I'm pretty sure it's not going to happen with her. I don't care what she says about hanging in there with her.

Enter Theresa. She would get involved with me today. I mean, I could call her now, while I'm driving back, and ask to see her tonight, and I bet we could wake up in the same bed in the morning if I let it go there. Guaranteed. But that would completely change our relationship, and I don't want to risk trashing it.

But that's nothing compared to what happened this afternoon with Jeannie. I saw her, really saw her for the first time. Jeannie, if you wanted to be seen as a woman, mission accomplished! You add that to the obvious talent you have for capturing emotion in your photography . . . as my mom told me after meeting you for the first time, the young man who captures your heart is going to be one lucky guy. I know you will chose well, Jeannie Irwin.Who knows what someday might bring?

Marcus's phone rang. He picked it up from the passenger seat, keeping his eyes on the road, then glanced quickly out of the corner of his eyes. Anna's picture was on the screen. He decided to let voicemail pick it up. He could listen in a few miles when he pulled over for a rest break.

Marcus took the exit ramp to the rest stop plaza and parked at the convenience store. He picked up his phone, leaving the car running and the air conditioning on, and went to his voicemail. He tapped Anna's message, "Hey, Marcus, call me tonight after nine. I know you want to talk more about us, and I just had too many things on my mind today. I'm sorry I cut you short. OK? Bye."

"Well, this should be interesting," Marcus said out

loud to himself as he turned the car off.

* * *

Marcus sat on a park bench looking westward over the Arkansas River. The last rays of the setting sun faded over the horizon spraying streaks of orange rays into a cloudless sky. The park behind him was clearing out. A few walkers and joggers lingered in the hot July night. Marcus, still heavy with sweat from an evening run up the trail and back, sipped from his water bottle. He eyed the phone resting on the bench beside him. The run helped calm him before his scheduled call with Anna.

This call could go either way. Am I ready for whatever happens? Something's gotta give. I can't let it eat on me because it's draining my emotional energy from so many other things. OK, Marcus, this conversation needs to happen, come what may. "Here goes, " Marcus said out loud.

The phone rang only twice, "Hi, Marcus, I've been waiting for your call," Anna's voice had a soft, compassionate tone. Like the way you talk to your dog as you drive him to the vet to put him down.

"I was disappointed that I didn't get more private time with you this weekend, and I guess it showed," Marcus began.

"You didn't have much to say when you left the rally. Kind of like you were in a rush to leave," Anna said.

Marcus pivoted, "I am glad I got a chance to meet Senator Manning. I've admired her ever since I was in college."

"And you got your picture taken with her, too," Anna interjected.

"Yes, I did. That was an unexpected pleasure. I've only seen her on TV, and I didn't realize she was so short."

"But she's a dynamo, isn't she? She knows how to get things done," Anna added.

"And I do see why you are impressed with Greer. He was very kind to give me so much personal time this morning. I did pick up some things from him."

"Yeah? What made the biggest impression?" Anna inquired.

"If you are not promoting change, you are not leading," Marcus said without hesitation.

"Life is a continual state of change for sure," Anna said then paused. "Marcus, I did not mean to cut you so short at the café this morning. I'm sorry. I don't–"

"You don't have to apologize," Marcus interrupted.

Anna continued, "Just the same, I don't want to give you the impression that I'm not interested in being with you. You are an amazing man in every way, and my affections for you run deep. That hasn't changed."

"But something has, Anna. I can feel it," Marcus countered.

Anna paused. "It's the timing. The timing. That's all,"

"Help me understand that, Anna."

"A lot has changed since we met—for both of us. Both of us have gone through changes at work that affected us personally. I thought I knew exactly what I wanted last October. Then the campaign happened. Now a whole new world of possibilities is opening up for me that I had not expected."

"I know what you mean about that," Marcus interjected.

"I thought that I wanted to be a corporate lawyer, and I was willing to work hard to be the best at that I could be. To make partner someday. Now, I've seen how important our political process is and how it works. I think

I have a future in immigration law with that issue being so hot and all. It's also a way for me to be the role model I always intended to be to my family and the young girls I can influence in my culture. I'm not sure where that will take me. I just know that I have to give myself the best opportunity I can for that to happen," Anna explained. "Senator Manning talked about how important women are in the political system and fighting for justice and equal rights and human rights. That spoke to me—inspired me. I want to be part of that. That's what I want, Marcus. What do you want?"

Marcus was silent briefly, "I want to have a family and roots like my parents and like Lauren and Jarod. I see how successful and amazingly happy they are, and that's what I want, too," Marcus confessed.

"And I believe you should have exactly what you want, dearest Marcus. You know it's time for that to happen for you. Right?" Anna pushed the point.

"Yes. Yes I do," Marcus admitted. Both remained silent for a few seconds before Marcus asked, "Does this mean we are breaking up? Going separate ways?"

Anna stayed silent. Several seconds passed before Anna continued softly, "In my law practice I have learned that when people are not getting what they need, want, or expected, they automatically go into a state of conflict. Sometimes it's very emotional and explosive. That's all conflict is—the difference between what we want and what we are getting. When that happens, there are two ways to resolve that conflict. First, you can get what you want, or second, you can adjust your expectations so that you are OK with what you are getting. I think we are at that place in deciding where this relationship goes."

"So, you are saying that because our individual ex-

> ## "Conflict is the difference between what we want and what we are getting."

pectations have changed since we met, that for one of us to get what they want the other has to give up what they want?" Marcus questioned.

"Think what would happen if we married anyway knowing what we know now. Then when we hit this crossroads, which inevitably we would, we would lose a spouse and create all kinds of additional anger, resentment, and hurt when the marriage failed over irreconcilable differences. As it is, we would be allowing each other, out of mutual respect and affection, to pursue their own dream. To bring expectations and reality into alignment," Anna reasoned.

"I know that all sounds all logical and reasonable the way you say it, but it breaks my heart just at the thought of letting you go," Marcus confessed, choking back a lump starting to form in his throat.

"I know. That's the emotional part. In our case, it's not what we have, because we haven't gone all the way, but it's what we are projecting we might have. No doubt, we care for each other. And to be honest with each other, we have to acknowledge that, if someday either, or both, of us is going to have something real and lasting, we have to let go of an illusion of what we hope, or think, we want to happen . . . but in reality cannot. That's what I mean,"

Anna finished.

"So," Marcus hesitated, sighed, and started again, "So, I repeat. Are we breaking up?".

"I Think of it," Anna pause. "I think of it," she caught herself, "We, we should think of it as allowing each other to become the best version of themselves without having to contort our dreams to fit someone else's mold. You want a family and roots, and I realize now that's nowhere in my plans for the foreseeable future, and to be honest, maybe ever," Anna confessed. She waited for Marcus to respond, and when he didn't, she added, "I believe it's the right thing to do—to let you have the future you want, and to wish you my love in finding it with the person who wants that same future with you."

"Why do you think this is the right time to make that call, Anna?"

"Because, on the Fourth, I saw the way you are with your family. I adore your family, especially Andy and Susie. Andy's already over me. He's infatuated with Jeannie. I know you are in your element with them, and I don't want to get in the way of any of that. It's too special."

"This is not what I want to hear," Marcus paused, struggling to compose himself, "but I respect your honesty. I thought in April you had a thing for Greer. Now I know you didn't. I was obsessing at times over something I was just making up in my head. I feel a little foolish about that. Thanks for being honest with me now," Anna started to speak, but Marcus cut her off. "And you're right, I can't move on to something else while clinging to an illusion. Better to be real about it," Marcus conceded.

"I'm glad you see it that way," Anna paused. "But, Marcus, keep me posted on how things are going. OK?"

"Yeah, sure," Marcus wanted this call to be over. The

finality of what was happening began to sink in.

"I'm sure Erin will fill me in about your work. I'll leave it up to you to tell me anything else you want me to know,"

"Yeah, sure."

"When you call, I'll always answer," Anna offered.

Marcus knew he would never call. "OK. I hope you find all the happiness you deserve, too." Marcus stopped there, feeling another lump welling up from his heart.

"And one thing more, Marcus. Be careful with Jeannie. It was so obvious to me that she is infatuated with you right now. You are her prince. I know how impressionable a young girl can be with a slightly older man—especially one like you, who has so much to offer. She needs time to grow up and to come into her own. Respect her, as I'm sure you will."

"Yeah, I promise," Marcus assured, wanting nothing of her advice at this point.

"Be well, dearest Marcus. I expect great things from you. Bye." Anna concluded.

Anna's last comment sounded to Marcus like when the boss tells you you're fired, then says that it's not personal. *Right now I just want to tell her she's a cold, aloof bitch and that I had sex with a Miss America runner-up, but that would only make me sound like a jerk.* Marcus replied with a matter-of-fact, and borderline terse, "Bye," and ended the connection. The disappointment he had been choking back erupted in uncontrollable sobs.

Just like that, it was over.

11. Celebrating

Monday morning, Marcus walked into the lab at 6:30 a.m. Only the soft breath of the air conditioning ruffled the silence. It would be a hot one today—triple digits. The oblique rays of the sun penetrated the lab casting elongated shadows past whatever got in the way. Marcus walked briskly into his office, tossed his satchel on the side chair, and lowered the shades to disperse the sunlight. *Glad to get back to some form of normal. Seems like a month since last Tuesday.*

Marcus picked up the framed photo of him, Anna, and Andy from last Halloween that he kept on the corner of his desk and let his eyes retrace the features of Anna's face. The heartache was real, and the lump in his chest tried to force its way up his throat, but Marcus took a deep breath and released it in a quivering sigh leaving his eyes moist. He opened a desk drawer to put the photo out of sight, then had second thoughts and closed the drawer leaving the photo in place. *Maybe later,* Marcus thought, hesitating. "Oh, what the hell," he said out loud and put the photo into the drawer. "That's that," Marcus wiped both eyes with the back of his hand, planted himself at his desk, and powered on the computer. *Better see where we are.*

Everyone had the Fourth off. Most had taken two days of annual leave, as he had, to make it a long weekend, since there was no immediate crisis in the lab. There had been no urgent emails or text messages from the team, and frankly, Marcus had been so preoccupied with what was going on with both Jeannie and Anna that he had not given work a second thought for nearly a week. Now, it was all he wanted to think about—not Jeannie, and now, not Anna.

The numbness that crept in Saturday night after the call with Anna, the final call of their relationship, dragged into Sunday. He slept late. He did not shave or shower, and this morning, he decided to skip shaving again. *Maybe I'll let my beard grow and see what happens. Maybe I'll take an early vacation and drive up into the Rockies. Maybe I'll even go backpacking. Never done that before, always thought I would like it.*

I wonder if Erin knows yet? Theresa called twice yesterday, but didn't feel like answering. Don't think I'll tell Theresa about the breakup with Anna. I know all that's holding her back from a full court press on me is my relationship with Anna. I don't want Theresa to be a rebound. I owe her better. I owe myself better. Maybe in a few days I'll tell her. Right now, keep up the façade that all is well. That's the plan.

Today, I want to talk with the team about the changes we've been going through the past month. I'm getting ready to be more involved with the company leadership project. I'm expecting that I'll be more involved with HR for the next two months if they are going to roll something out after Labor Day. I want to make sure everyone knows what to expect and that we have a plan for our projects. We should have a team conversation about all the changes we've faced since February.

Marcus's phone chimed. Theresa. A text this time. "saw your car in lot. Hot tea in the cafe? I'm buying."

Why not? he thought. *I don't want to avoid her entire-*

ly. "Sure. See you in a min," Marcus replied.

Marcus approached the beverage kiosk in the Black Gold Café only to see Theresa already situated at a table by the windows where she could watch for him. She waved him over. He could see a cup with a tea bag steeping already waiting for him.

"I know you like lemon ginger tea in the morning," Theresa wore a white short sleeve cotton blouse showing off her even, caramel tan that set off her sun-bleached blond hair, giving her that California-girl look. Today, she let it drop over her shoulders—a departure from the bun she usually wore at work.

"This is a new look at work for you," Marcus greeted Theresa.

"And you're sporting a new look this morning, too," Theresa rubbed her chin, noting Marcus's stubble.

"Felt like a change of pace," Marcus offered, taking his seat. "Thanks for getting the tea ready."

"You mean a change of face," Theresa giggled. "I kind of like scruffy," she teased. "What happened to bring this on?"

"Nothing. Just wondered what it would feel like to try something different."

"Well, did you have a good weekend? Since you didn't return my calls, I thought you might be otherwise . . . preoccupied?" Theresa ended in a mysterious tone, raising her eyebrows and tilting her head as if to pose a question.

It took a second for Theresa's innuendo to sink in, "Oh," Marcus exclaimed when it hit him what Theresa suggested, "No, no, n-o-o-o-o-o, nothing like that. Just a normal family weekend," Marcus's voice trailed off, then he perked up with a smile, "My sister, Emily, is pregnant. That was the big news that got everyone excited."

"Well, that would do it. Congratulations. So you're going to be an uncle all over again."

"Yep. Yep. I've very excited for them," Marcus took a sip, "It's their first," his eyes darted side to side avoiding direct contact with Theresa, then, changed the subject, "How about you, what did you end up doing?"

"Not much. Went with friends to the fireworks along the river. Then, worked the rest of the week. No reason to take any time off. Hit the farmers market early Saturday morning," Theresa paused, then pressed, "Are you sure you're telling me everything? You're acting kind of funny—evasive."

"Met Eric Greer Saturday morning. Went to a political rally. Anna is all ga-ga over it, and I guess I'm bothered a little by all that," Marcus lied.

"Are you suspicious?"

"No. Not really. I mean, I met Greer's fiancée, Renee. She's gorgeous, outgoing, just the type for a millionaire politician. Don't think Greer would stray from that. It's just that Anna's so into the political scene. I felt edged out," Marcus added.

"I'd be happy to take your mind off it later this week if you'd like to come over for dinner," Theresa offered.

"Maybe. At least maybe we could go out for dinner. We'll see. There's a lot of changes going on at work, and I'm a little overwhelmed, that's all," Marcus dodged.

"Speaking of changes, Marcus. I got some interesting news Friday," Theresa confessed. She wiggled in her chair and scooted up more erect, placing her forearms on the table, her fingertips interlaced in front of her.

"Oh? Looks like it was good news. Am I right?"

"Good news. Yes." Theresa leaned in, "I'm getting a promotion. Gonna be a supervisor as of the fifteenth,"

Theresa was all smiles.

"Oh, my, how wonderful. And you're just now telling me?" Marcus exclaimed sincerely jubilant and leaning forward mirroring Theresa's posture.

"Actually, when I was told late Friday afternoon, the first thing I wanted to do was call you. I was so excited and couldn't wait to share it. But I knew you were with family and—everything, so I waited until Sunday. I wanted to tell you in person, but you didn't pick up my calls."

"Sorry about that, but in that case, I want to take you out for a celebration tonight. Just you and me at Tulsa's finest."

"I'd love that," Theresa eagerly accepted.

"We'll dress up and really celebrate. Pull out all the stops. White tablecloth type of place, ritzy, elegant atmosphere, classy," Marcus's excitement grew as he spoke.

"Love it. Just us. OK?" Theresa confirmed.

"You got it. I'm so proud of you. In the meantime, I've got to get to the lab," Marcus shifted his weight, getting ready to stand.

"I've got a stack of work on my desk, too," Theresa added, "and I've got to decide what to wear tonight."

"And I'll have to clean up," Marcus grinned stroking his two-day old stubble with the top of his curled fingers.

"Don't do it on my account," Theresa said. "It makes you look," she paused, then through a mischievous grin, teased, "playful." And struck out preceding Marcus toward the café exit.

Marcus followed her, noticing how she moved when she walked, causing a momentary flash back on how she flowed from couple to couple at Lizzie's Memorial weekend cookout. Marcus smiled to himself and realized he was actually feeling—playful. The thought seeped into his mind, Anna who? *Maybe letting go will be easier than I expected.*

Marcus was back in the lab at 7:45. He could hear the chatter from the break area in the far corner. The lab looked like it was waking up after a period of hibernation. Marcus sensed a fresh energy. Maybe it was just him and the lift Theresa's good news gave him.

Of course Sanjar, the team's wannabe cowboy storyteller, captivated everyone with the adventurous recounting of his weekend. Marcus walked in on the story mid-telling. Sanjar saw him coming.

"Marcus, Marcus, please come. I was just getting to the good part, the most exciting part. After the fireworks at the river I was walking back to my truck with my friends, and as I stepped out on Riverside Drive a car shot out from a parking lot and slammed on the brakes stopping just short of hitting me. The driver leaned out the window to apologize, and there she was. I walked over to tell her all was OK. She was horrified that she nearly hit me. She was trembling. She put her hand on the edge of her door, and in an instant, a reflex really, I reached down and put my hand on the top of hers, and in a magical moment our eyes met, and I knew she was destined to be mine. I told her all was well, and I would like to buy her and her friend a drink to show no harm done. She agreed, we hit it off, and then we went dancing Friday night and spent most of the weekend together. Marcus, I know how you must have felt when you first met your Anna," Sanjar took a breath.

"Well?" Miranda, one of the technicians pleaded, "What's her name?"

"Oh, yes, of course," Sanjar continued, "Her name

is Angela. She prefers Angie. She's from Austin, Texas. She's up visiting a college friend. She grew up on a ranch, and her parents and two younger brothers still work it. She still barrel races at rodeos sometimes. She's a real cowgirl. A—real—cowgirl!" he repeated, emphasizing each word. "The girl of my dreams. Can you believe it? My life has changed. I am so happy."

Sue Ann, who was standing next to Sanjar, hugged him, "I'm happy for you, Sanjar. I hope she really is the one."

Marcus added, "Yes, I know the feeling, Sanjar, and I'm happy for you, too. I hope it lasts a lifetime." Then Marcus changed the subject, "I bet we all have stories, but we have to take some time to get reorganized first thing this morning. How about we have our usual 8:30 meeting?"

Everyone agreed, and Marcus headed back to his office. *I think some time for reflection from the group might be helpful in our meeting today. We don't have any major crisis facing us, so maybe it's time to retrace our steps and revisit our experiences to see what we have learned from the changes we've been through.*

The team assembled right on time. Everyone brought notes and project files. Marcus looked around the group sitting in their usual places. Marcus realized he, too, had become accustomed to his chair at the far end with the whiteboard to his back and where he could see the door. *How quickly the comfort zone sets in,* Marcus thought. *Like the family around a dinner table, everyone has a place, and when they are absent, no one sits there. No need to take role.*

When Marcus was a new team leader he would sit in different places to deliberately mix things up. That didn't seem to be necessary now, and everyone settled into a space.

Marcus panned the room clockwise, starting on his left. Sue Ann Lee, a Korean/African American electrical engineer, sat to his immediate left. She was definitely overqualified in her staff technician position. Next to her was Lori Ellis, the team's mechanical wizard. Carlos Alvarez, a graduate of a turbine tech program, was a good liaison between the wind farm and the lab. Brad Skiver, one of the three engineers, sat at the corner of the table. He always had his chair scooted back slightly, like he really did not want to be there. Chris Daniels came next. He was the oldest of the technicians at thirty-five. A single parent with two children. Smart and extremely introverted. Miranda Evans, sat to Chris's left. She was talented in both electrical and electronics disciplines–much more talented than her resumé suggested. Dan Packwood, the elder statesman of the engineers was at the far corner. He was a stabilizing force in the lab. He could have been the team leader, but passed on the promotion. Sanjar Banai, born in the USA to affluent Indian immigrants, sat in the middle chair on his side of the table. Sanjar had made his way to Oklahoma in 2009 in search of the cowboy way of life complete with a cowgirl wife. Sanjar provided the comic relief for the team. Sierra Trammel, the third engineer, who with Dan had been on the team since it was formed in 2004, occupied the final chair, to Marcus's immediate right. *The last sixteen months have been a wild ride. A lot of changes. I think we are starting to gel. I hope that everything we've been through will help us deal with the changes I know are coming.*

Marcus began. "Is everyone as glad to get back to work as I am?" That met with mixed reaction. Marcus continued, "Dan, thanks for holding down the fort."

"It was quiet, and I got a lot of things cleaned up," Dan replied. "Besides, I'm glad I saved my leave. I'm going to need it." Dan suddenly had everyone's undivided attention. He paused for dramatic effect. "My daughter, Grace, announced she is getting married in December on New Years Eve, and I have a feeling I'm going to be heavily involved in the planning, because I'm the planner in the family, and because I'm picking up the tab."

The table erupted in laughter and congratulations for Dan. Marcus continued when the chatter settled, "Seems like there are a lot of changes going on for everyone, and that's why today I want to depart a little from our usual business-like approach. As a group we're problem solvers. We fix it and move on." Everyone nodded in agreement. "And we've gone through some pretty big changes the past eight or nine months. I thought we needed a session to think back how all this has affected us individually and as a team. So I want to open up the conversation and ask each of you to comment on any changes you have gone through that you are comfortable talking about."

Sanjar jumped in first, "Like meeting the perfect woman?" Everyone laughed. He continued, "But seriously, my decision to move to Tulsa is the most traumatic and rewarding move I ever made in my life. As you know, my father had very different plans for me. Our traditional customs in India about courtship and marriage were unacceptable to me. I wanted a different life than what I saw some of my family and friends had. I knew I had to find my own life; so, I announced I was leaving India and returning to the United States to take this job. Had it not been for my mother, I think my father would have disowned me. Working with this group has been a great joy. And now, I am in love with a real cowgirl, just as I imagined it would someday be."

"Do you have pictures to prove it?" Lori teased.

"Yes, I posted several on Facebook," Sanjar tapped his phone's screen a couple of times. "Here. See. My rodeo queen." Sanjar passed the phone around.

Sue Ann spoke up. "I'll go next. A big change for me began when we had to defend our project. Until then, I really enjoyed this job, but I felt sometimes like I was just going through the motions. I would come to work, do a good job, go home, repeat the next day, and so on. I think the funding crisis pulled us together. I was scared at first—the thought that we could lose our jobs. Then, as we started working more with each other, I saw our project from different perspectives, such as our vendors, field staff, and other departments in this company. I think we found new ways to work together because we were forced out of our comfort zones. As we went, I realized how much I was actually enjoying the challenge. In the end when Mr. Johnstone came to our lab—our lab," she emphasized, "I felt like we had won an Olympic gold medal, or something like that. I was so elated. And that

> *"We found new ways to work together because we were forced out of our comfort zones."*

inspired me, along with Dan's encouragement, to ask Marcus if I could facilitate our team review of the presentation. I know now that I can push my comfort zone a little at a time. I'm confident I will be in an engineer's position someday." Sue Ann caught herself, "of course, I don't mean that I'm trying to take any of our very capable engineer's jobs," she smiled, and everyone chuckled at her unnecessary apology.

Marcus stepped in, "Sanjar, Sue Ann, thanks for sharing. Those are good examples of how change is both scary and rewarding. And Sue Ann, I'm confident you will make an excellent engineer when the right opportunity comes along." Marcus continued. "I remember how scared I was just to tell you all about the funding issue. I was scared and disheartened and angry that we were broadsided that way. Sometimes change causes friction and things heat up. Like a fire, it can get out of control and destroy, or we can manage it and use it to our advantage. Thanks to all of you, we got that situation under control and came out of it better for the experience." Marcus looked around the table, "Who's next?"

Lori Ellis spoke up. "I've admired Sue Ann since we met. She's so smart, and I never got to go to college. I know you all probably didn't realize it, but I'd come to work wondering why I was here, that I didn't fit. The threat to our funding drew us closer as we worked to figure it out. I realized that I was smarter than I was giving myself credit for. The more we discussed each other's work and looked over it together, the more confident I was that I could hold my own here. I grew up taking things apart and putting them back together. I think I can hold my own in college and want to study mechanical engineering. So, I guess my change is similar to Sue Ann's."

"Good example, Lori," Marcus complimented. "It's good to see these positive changes happening for you. Are you going to enroll in any class this fall?"

"My husband is encouraging me to do it. He says the boys are old enough now that they don't need me doting over them. In fact, he says our eleven-year old could help me with my math," Lori laughed.

Chris Daniels, cleared his throat and leaned forward over the table, signaling he wanted to speak. He had a habit of sitting on his hands when he spoke, like he was restraining himself. Some say it is a sign of shyness, and Chris usually kept his thoughts close. Marcus gave him a nudge, "Chris, it looks like you have something to say."

"My example is kind of personal, I mean it's not entirely work related. Would that be OK?"

"Sure, Chris. Whatever you're comfortable with," Marcus encouraged.

"Well, I'm not totally comfortable with it, but I kind of feel like I should be more open about it since I'm not one to go on about my personal life. I just feel like we have been through a lot, especially since March, and I feel like I can open up a little more with you all." Chris looked around the table. Everyone sat quietly, all eyes on him, except Brad, who was glancing down at his phone, then looked up when he noticed everyone was quiet.

"So here goes," Chris continued. "You all know I'm a single dad. What you don't know is the story behind it. It's been hard for me to tell anyone, but I feel like I'm among friends, and I want you to hear it from me. Anyway, here goes."

Chris cleared his throat and began. "Kathy ran off to California with a guy she met somewhere, I don't know where. All she told me was how boring I am and a total embarrassment to the male species, as she called it. Said she didn't know she was marrying a nerd. Said I would die alone and bored. Of course, that's not true. I have the kids, Jake and Kate. Kathy said being a mother wasn't her idea of a good time, and I could have the kids. They'd probably just be nerds too, like me. The heartache and rejection of hearing that from someone who was supposed to love you was excruciating." Chris interlaced his fingers and squeezed them nervously, and then popped the knuckles on his index fingers.

"She convinced me all along that it was me. A real man made real money and could take care of his family. Then this job came along with better pay and benefits and opportunity. She left anyway."

Everyone sat riveted except Brad, who gave a jerky faint sigh of boredom, as if trying to hide it, then looked up realizing he had been detected, "Excuse me," he said, then looked down. Marcus nodded for Chris to continue.

"Anyway, like I was saying, the change. Obviously the kids and Kathy were big changes. Huge. But, the most amazing change was finding out how wrong she was. That I was a good dad, a devoted husband, smart . . . and interesting." Chris cracked a smile. "The big change, sort of a moment of clarity, was realizing that I had been living a lie, because I believed the lie. When I let go of it, everything changed.

"What I wanted to say about change is that sometimes we really don't need to change what we are doing, only what we think about it. In this case, I learned from teachers, parents of my kid's friends, coaches, friends at church and others, that what happened between me and Kathy wasn't on me alone, and maybe not at all. I had more than one moment of truth where I looked at the

> *"The big change, sort of a moment of clarity, was realizing that I had been living a lie, because I believed the lie. When I let go of it, everything changed."*

results of my actions and saw that everything I did, I did for my kids and family. I am trying to get outside myself, and my immediate family more and find interests. My photography has done that. I've joined a local photography club and made some new friends, even met a nice young lady, and who knows what all can happen now? Right Sanjar? My life was good, then bad, then awful, then it downright sucked, and now it's better. I came out on the other side a lot happier with myself. And I appreciate that you have let me be me, and have been my friends through it all." Chris put his hands together in a prayer gesture as if to say thank you, paused and dropped his eyes to the table.

A spontaneous applause broke out in the group. Even Brad made a half-hearted effort, so as not to be left out of a consensus gesture. Miranda, who was sitting next to Chris put her arm around his shoulder and squeezed him, then added, "Chris, I'm sorry you've carried such a burden by yourself. Even as quiet as you can be, I've never thought that you were boring. Besides, I know what it's like to interrupt your plans to take care of someone. I had to do that when my parents were injured in a car wreck. You're an awesome dad."

Sierra, in her mid-forties, whisked a tear with the tips of fingers, "Raising kids alone is tough," she spoke, clearing a lump in her throat. "My two were older when their dad was killed, but we got through it. I'm always here for you, Chris."

"We all are, Chris," Marcus added. "What this says to me is that we are getting a lot more comfortable being together, and that's a good sign that we trust each other more. And it shows me that your life can't be so easily compartmentalized. It has to be more integrated—work and home. I appreciate how everyone puts their shoulder to the wheel when necessary. I also want this to be a place where we can feel relaxed and confident that we've got each other's back. I know our best work is ahead of us. I'll do my part to help each and everyone of you to be the best you can be."

Marcus looked around the group again, "Anyone else?" No one offered, "Well, thanks, everyone. Our numbers are spot on for now. I know we all are tweaking our systems to keep efficiencies as high as possible. Keep up the good work. One more thing. As you all know, I've been assigned to work with HR on a new leadership program. I don't have a lot of details yet about my exact involvement, but I'd like to have a team huddle devoted to what adjustments we might need to make as the project unfolds. How do we keep things on track and make sure we stay on top of our game? So I'd appreciate it if you give it some thought and we'll discuss it next Monday. OK?"

All agreed. The team lingered for a moment then

shuffled out of the conference room. Even Brad lingered briefly to congratulate Sanjar on his new-found love, "We all should be so lucky," he said, offering a fist bump. Sanjar noticed the gesture immediately and responded accompanying the bump with a beaming smile.

Marcus's phone chimed—a message from Erin, "can u come up at 1:30?"

"yes" Marcus replied. *She knows*, he thought, *Anna must have called her.*

"Marcus," Dan's voice snapped Marcus from his momentary trance. Marcus looked up to acknowledge him. "Just wanted to say how much I appreciated the last hour. Some might think this conversation was just idle chat, but I can tell how much this group has come together since March. Talks like this help us connect. I think we're really starting to click. You can count on me to step up anyway you need me. OK?"

"Sure, Dan. OK. I appreciate it. Thanks."

Dan nodded and headed to his office.

Marcus paused and selected Theresa in his message list, "can't make lunch. pick u up at 7."

A few seconds later from Theresa, "can't wait."

Better make that reservation, Marcus thought, that giddy, playful feeling rushed over him again.

The message alert chimed on Marcus's phone. Whitney. Marcus remembered she had to work over the weekend to help debug the software migration at her billing company. Hope her weekend went better than mine.

"Migration smoother than expected. My homemade training helped. My team had fewer problems than others during transition. Word got around to other teams from my associates. They shared lessons I developed with friends and so on. Other supervisors were complimentary. My supervisor, not so much. Said I probably violated some copyright laws taking screenshots without prior approval. Told me this morning to back off until legal could check it out. But hey, no good deed goes unpunished. Drama, drama. Later."

Marcus replied, "Hang in there. Call me later this week with follow up. Change makers are risk takers."

Marcus started into his office, then paused, turned and walked to Brad's office, stopping at the door. Brad sat with his back to the door holding his phone, but not talking on it. Marcus knocked against the doorframe to announce his presence, and Brad swiveled around. "May I come in?" Marcus asked.

"Looks like you already have," Brad laid his phone on the desk and leaned back in his chair. He looked annoyed and sighed. "What's on your mind?"

Marcus ventured another step farther onto Brad's turf. "During the year I've been team lead, I just feel that we haven't got comfortable with each other. I'd like to close any distance between us. I thought maybe it's time we just talked about it," Marcus began.

"Is there anything wrong with my work?" Brad asked.

"No. I'm OK with your job performance."

"Then, there's no problem as far as I'm concerned," Brad said matter-of-factly.

"Don't you think there's something to be said for the

Change makers are risk takers.

esprit de corps of the group?" Marcus asked.

"Not really. Everyone knows I'll do my part completely, on time, and right. That's all that matters to me. I
didn't grow up a jock playing on teams, high-fiving, and
slapping butts. I did my schoolwork, kept my nose clean,
made the grades, got scholarships, and graduated at the
top of my class. I'm a damn good engineer, and frankly,
I couldn't give a rat's ass whether you and I have an *esprit de corps* kind of guy relationship, or some Kumbaya
whatever that was we just did. So if you don't mind, I
have some reports to double check."

Brad's vituperative retort slapped at Marcus's sensi-
bilities. He choked back his first impulse to lash out in
defense. *OK Marcus, you've been suspecting this. Maybe
this was a bad idea to ask here in Brad's office, but I guess
there's no time like the present to deal with this. First,
deflect and redirect. Don't get suckered into an argument.
Acknowledge Brad's tone, or anger. Affirm his feelings,
then state what you want to be the best possible outcome
for this conversation. And Breathe.*

"I know, Brad, you haven't gone out of the way to
act friendly toward me. I also know you have not directly challenged my authority either, which I appreciate. I
agree that there is no rule that you have to like me. I'm
glad to know how you intend to act toward me and this
team, so I won't spend too much energy hoping for anything different. All I expect is for you to treat everyone on
this team with the respect and dignity they deserve. And
remember the principle that you tend to get back what
you give out. I promise I will treat you the way I want you
to treat me. Fair enough?" Marcus stood looking down at
Brad.

"Fair enough," Brad replied. "Now if you'll excuse

me." Brad swiveled around, turning his back to Marcus.

Marcus paused, seething. *You arrogant shit.* Marcus headed back to his office. He was keenly aware of his shallow breathing and that it took all the restraint he could muster to contain his anger and desire to lash out at Brad. *So, Brad just confirmed what I had suspected. I doubt his attitude will ever change. I have to be sure that I don't give him any ammunition. I can never manage Brad's attitude, but I can mine. OK, Marcus, don't let that jerk get under your skin. Think about something plesant instead. Like going out tonight with Theresa.*

* * *

Erin met Marcus in the foyer of her office suite, "Come in Marcus, I wanted to catch up with you about all the changes going on with you and your team. Just want to make sure you're OK."

"There have been some changes, all right," Marcus agreed. "In fact, this morning my team talked about how those changes have affected them."

"Good. That's an important conversation to have every once in a while. Change can just creep up on us and we don't notice how it affects us."

"And some times it kicks the door down," Marcus added as he and Erin entered her office and took seats around her conference table.

"How is the leadership project is going?"

"I think I'm about to get more involved. HR wants to roll out the first classes after Labor Day."

"And I fully support that project and your involvement in it. What adjustments are you making with your team to make sure they have what they need since your attention will be elsewhere?"

"We talked about that today, actually. Dan offered to step up, and I told the team that at our next staff meeting I would like to hear their suggestions about how they could help each other. I think we're going to be OK for now," Marcus explained.

"It sounds like your group has everything under control. An effective team is adaptable."

"So, you're comfortable with how I'm handling everything?" Marcus asked. He didn't bring up the conversation with Brad.

"Yes, of course. You've been through a lot since October. I'm pleased with your resilience and the way you've become stronger from the adversity you've been through."

"The trip to Montana was an eye-opener. I know Jim Bob is a great drilling engineer, but I could see how the crews were on guard around him. I don't think he saw it. They all treated me well, even though I got a lot of friendly ribbing about chasing windmills. They call me Wind Boy," Marcus chuckled as he explained the nickname.

"On guard around him?" Erin asked, inviting Marcus to say more.

"He obviously knows drilling, but I saw him go off on some of the crew because they were having trouble with a well. He kind of put them down, you know."

"That's too bad. What else did you pick up?"

"But he's not always like that," Marcus added hastily, remembering Jim Bob with Patti and the events at Outfitters. "I don't think he's as tough as he likes to act. The crews work hard, and there's a bond among them. The work is hard, and the hours are long. Conditions can be extreme. They are committed. Drilling is their life. My impression is that they see no end to our dependence on oil and gas," Marcus offered.

"Have you had any more contact with Jim Bob?"

"No. I think we came to a mutual respect. He still thinks wind is a fool's game. I invited him to see our Burns Flat field, but he didn't seem interested."

"Well, things change regardless of whether you want to accept it, or not," Erin said.

"You know I didn't ask for any of the changes that are happening to me lately? Right?" Marcus stated.

"Sometimes change finds us, and tests us to see what we are made of," Erin added.

"Tell me about it. I'm glad you support the opportunity I have with this HR project," Marcus said. "I'm actually enjoying the challenge. I want to see where this all goes. Do you have any advice?"

"Well, you might not be as involved in the day-to-day of your team, but you still are responsible for supporting them. You've got to make sure they are clear about their goals, that they have the tools and resources they need to do their job, and that they have a clear plan for their work," Erin offered.

"That I can do," Marcus agreed.

"Good. If you ever have any problems, or think you are going to have problems, I want to be the first to know so I can help you through them. No matter what," Erin affirmed.

"Will do."

Erin smiled and her voice softened, signaling a change in subject, "I also wanted to ask how you are after the weekend? Anna called and told me everything."

Marcus dropped his gaze to the table top which sported several industry journals neatly cascading one on top of another, "It was hard hearing that she didn't see a future for us," Marcus got serious, then stopped.

"I'm sorry, but I'm sure she didn't intend to hurt you."

"I know she didn't. After I thought about it, I can see why her professional goals are at odds with my personal needs," Marcus offered.

"Anna has some specific expectations for her future. She sees some new opportunities possible for her that will likely take her farther away from Springfield," Erin added.

"Life happens, I guess. We just have to evolve with it," Marcus looked into Erin's eyes and paused.

"And there will be more changes down the road. I want you to know I'll help you every way I can," Erin offered.

"I'm sure I'll be needing it," Marcus suddenly wished the conversation would end. "Is there anything else?"

"No. I guess not. I just wanted to check in to make sure you are OK," Erin sounded sympathetic.

"Thanks," Marcus looked Erin in the eyes and offered a half smile.

"Good. I know how much she really cares for you too," Erin smiled as she stood.

Marcus stood in the door, "I better get back."

---

*"Sometimes change finds us
and tests us to see what
we're made of."*

---

12. A surprising reflection

Marcus rang Theresa's doorbell and nervously fidgeted with the knot of his tie. He noticed the wooden door slightly ajar behind the full-length glass storm door, common on Tulsa homes. A few seconds passed. Marcus hear movement inside. He was keenly aware of his sweaty palms and shallow, rapid breathing that had come on as he approached the front door.

Gosh, Marcus, this is silly. Why are you so nervous about this? It isn't really a date. Or is it? Maybe it's that I really do want this to be a date. Maybe I've been attracted to Theresa all along and just didn't want to be a jerk dating two women at the same time, like I would be cheating on both of them at once. Now Anna has broken things off, so I have no reason to feel uncomfortable with this. Except that this could get serious quickly and go totally south if I'm not careful and sure of myself and my feelings about Theresa. Damn, don't over think this. Anna cut you loose—remember. Enjoy Theresa, and don't be afraid of your feelings about her.

The wooden door pulled open. Theresa stepped into view. "Come in, Marcus."

Marcus gasped at his first glance of Theresa, but he had no apprehensions as he did with Jeannie at her front door. Theresa had styled her sun-bleached blonde hair into a windblown updo. She wore a wine red sleeveless lace sheath dress with a scalloped hemline just below her knees. It showed her shape and gave her golden tan an exotic glow. Her finger nails and toenails were a deep red shade, slightly brighter than the dress. Her necklace and earrings a deep red garnet to match. Marcus pulled the glass door open, and as he entered he handed her a bouquet of spring flowers. "You look ravishing," Marcus spoke as Theresa took the flowers.

"How sweet of you. Come in and let's get these in a vase." She took the bouquet as Marcus stepped into the foyer, letting her hands gently cup both the flowers and Marcus's hand that held them, all the while holding eye contact. Marcus was awkwardly aware of how transfixed he was at the sight of Theresa.

Theresa turned into the living room, pivoting slowly keeping eye contact until her body forced her head to follow around. Marcus caught her fragrance and paused to take in the slightest hint of what he thought to be lilac. The dress elongated her lines. She seemed to flow. He followed without speaking, and he stopped in the kitchen doorway and watched. Theresa reached into the pantry and brought out a vase and filled it. Her tanned arms were more toned than Marcus had noticed.

"The flowers are lovely," Theresa said sniffing them before removing the plastic wrapper and arranging them in the vase. "Flowers make me feel happy. I love the colors."

Marcus watched, *She's more beautiful than I ever noticed. Fuller and more fit than I thought. She has a natural gracefulness about her. Elegant, mesmerizing.*

"That should do it," Theresa said placing the flowers in the center of her dining table and turning on the light above it causing the flowers to look like they were on display. "That way when we come in tonight, I'll see them first thing to remind me of this wonderful evening we are about to enjoy."

"I hope you like my choice of restaurants. We'll be dining at the Lilac Garden," Marcus said.

"Oh, wonderful," Theresa expressed an excited surprise. "I've heard about it, but haven't had the pleasure yet. I was kind of hoping you would pick someplace like that, so I took a chance and dressed for it. Do you think this is too much?" Theresa turned side to side in place showing both profiles and placing her hand on her hip each time as if she were modeling her dress.

"Perfect. You're absolutely perfect," Marcus approved. "Shall we?" Marcus invited, gesturing toward the front door.

"Yes. Let's," Theresa smiled and walked up to Marcus and, with the back of her curled fingers stroked his still unshaven chin and left cheek, gazing with her liquid blue eyes into his. Then repeated the motion with her left hand on his right cheek, taking her time and tilting her head to each side as she surveyed his three-day-old beard. "Hmmmm, Good," she said with that mischievous smile, took his hand and led him to the front door, picking up her black sequined clutch purse on the way.

Marcus maneuvered his Z through the ongoing road construction in Tulsa's emerging arts and entertainment district of reclaimed and rehabilitated warehouses north of downtown. Investors were returning to downtown to match other inner cities vying for Millennials who preferred an urban lifestyle. Several buildings had been renovated with first floor retail space and the upper floors converted into affordable apartments and lofts. Several buildings were devoted to small offices. There were rumors of a former car dealership location that would be built out for entrepreneurs needing shared space to get a start. A new ballpark opened a couple of years earlier to keep its minor league franchise happy. Crowds were returning to the district, and with them, bars, boutique coffee shops, and cafes. The Lilac Garden was the only fine dining establishment so far, and there was usually a waiting list for the limited seating and elegant and intimate atmosphere. It had quickly become the place for love struck men of all ages to propose marriage.

Marcus was eager to show Theresa a good time to congratulate her on her promotion and to show his gratitude for all she had done to support him since meeting her in February. He had the feeling that it was going to be something more. And he welcomed the change.

Marcus pulled up to the valet parking attendant in front of the Lilac Garden. The attendants scurried to open the doors for both driver and passenger. They knew how to make an impression on their discerning patrons. Marcus walked around to the sidewalk and offered Theresa his arm and escorted her to the front door, which was being held by a greeter.

"Welcome to the Lilac Garden," a tall young woman in a sleek black after five dress and perfectly styled long black hair and immaculate makeup said, motioning them inside with her left arm, palm up, her tapered fingers pointing to the foyer. The maître d' stood erect at his station, "Good evening, welcome to the Lilac Garden."

"Reservations for Winn, please," Marcus offered.

"Yes, Mr. Winn. I see this is a special occasion tonight? A celebration for Ms. Younger?"

"Yes, that's correct," Marcus confirmed

"And I also see, Mr. Winn, this is your first time to dine with us?"

"Yes," Marcus smiled. Theresa squeezed Marcus's hand slightly when he said, "yes."

"I have a special table for you in a corner. Jessie will escort you. Enjoy."

The hostess unfolded the napkins for both Theresa and Marcus and placed them in their laps. She took their drink orders, and excused herself after informing them their waiter would be Robert.

"Marcus, this is exquisite," Theresa was delighted. The softened light made Theresa look even more radiant. The dress shimmered, the highlights of her blonde hair looked like rays of sun streaming from her beaming face of blue eyes and irrepressible smile.

"You look happy," Marcus observed.

"I am, I am," Theresa repeated herself. "Right now, this very moment, is the happiest I can remember being for a long time." Theresa paused, then continued, "Marcus, I can't tell you how many times I've imagined an evening like this with you, and now," Theresa looked around wide-eyed taking in the scene, becoming part of the ambiance herself, then back into Marcus's eyes, "and now, here I am, here we are, just you and me, not at work, or a substitute date. This night, this moment is just us, celebrating happiness." Theresa sighed, dropping her chin, then smiled demurely as she glanced back up to Marcus, then sighed with a pout, "except for those darned boundaries."

A spontaneous boyish smile and a blush washed over Marcus. He wanted to tell her about Anna, but chose to stay focused on Theresa. "You know, in all the months I've known you, I haven't heard you talk about your past. All I really know is you're from California," Marcus invited her story.

Theresa looked down. Her expression grew more somber, "Those times weren't so happy." She looked back up,

"I guess I should just tell you and get it out of the way."

"I didn't mean to bring you down. I–"

Theresa cut it off. "No. It's OK. California, yes. Born in Santa Rosa, in the Napa region," Theresa smoothed out the tablecloth in front of her with the fingertips of both hands as she began. "An only child. When I was ten, we moved to Los Angeles where my dad could make a better living. He worked in the beverage industry. But what I remember most is how unhappy my parents were together. They argued constantly. I remember wanting to play at my friend's so I wouldn't have to listen to them. And I made friends easily, because if I had friends I had someplace else to go besides home." Theresa rolled her eyes and looked up at the ceiling like she was visualizing a scene from that time. "Anyway," Theresa looked down and away, "they went through an ugly divorce my senior year." She paused, then re-established eye contact with Marcus, "I always wanted a home like my friend's.

"Then I started college at Glendale Community College. I wanted to be a psychologist, I thought, or a counselor. I met a couple of young guys starting out. They were building an event planning business, and they offered me a job. They said I had the personality for it. As it turned out, I had a knack for the business, too. Soon I was bringing in business of my own–and a lot of it. I got my associate degree, but by that time the business was really happening, and I found myself in a relationship with Evan, one of the owners. We moved in together.

"Then one day I found out that Evan, who was the eighty percent partner, secretly agreed to sell the business for a big profit. The new owners didn't want his staff, but he managed to save his own hide. He threw everyone else under the bus. 'Just business,' he said. Anyway, that was that. I got a lawyer and sued. Evan settled, and I walked away with enough money to start over. I did odd jobs for a few years and saved every penny I could scrape together. I couldn't get past the betrayal.

"A friend I had made in class told me about Tulsa, where she was from, and said it would be a good place to start over, real friendly, uncomplicated, and so not California. It sounded refreshing. So, sight unseen, I picked up and moved. No job, no nothing. Happened onto the house I'm living in. My real estate agent told me she knew someone who worked at Johnstone and thought I could get a job there. And I did, and, as it turned out, I had a knack for it," Theresa looked directly into Marcus's eyes and smiled, "And here I am." Then, she gave her a head a slight tilt to the right and a shrug as if to say, "That's all folks."

Robert came to the table with menus, a server accompanied him with their drinks. He offered the specials for the evening and left Marcus and Theresa to make their selections.

"That's some story, Theresa. Those were some pretty disruptive changes. Thanks for sharing it." Marcus picked up his wine glass and held it up, inviting Theresa to do likewise, which she did, "Here's to your success and happiness in Tulsa." They tapped glasses and sipped.

The dinner and service that accompanied it was four-star. Theresa's joyfulness resurfaced. The conversation recapped their time together at work, the morning they met in the Black Gold Café, Marcus's frequent appearances at Theresa's lunch table in the cafeteria, her ongoing presence to support him, and readiness to stand in for Anna when needed.

Marcus noticed every move and gesture Theresa

made. He traced the contours of her face, the shape of her mouth and texture of her lips, the way she held her glass and the way her mouth caressed its rim when she sipped, the way she handled the silverware with her tapered fingers that were both delicate and strong. Her laugh had a lively resonance that invited one to want to laugh with her. The mellow, alto quality of her voice could sound sultry and seductive when she spoke softly. He imagined what her breathy, whispered invitation to explore her more intimately would sound like and feel like in his ear. The nape of his neck and the backs of his ears tingled at the thought. When plates were cleared from the entrée, Theresa laid her right had on the table. Marcus wanted to reach for it, but held back.

Robert approached the table with desserts and champagne, "Compliments of the Lilac Garden, on your promotion, Ms. Younger." Robert replaced the wine glasses with champagne flutes and poured the sparkling beverage that fizzed as it filled. Theresa giggled delightfully.

Marcus picked up his glass and held it again to toast. Theresa mirrored Marcus's gesture. "Theresa, to your accomplishments, your continued success, and your happiness." They tapped their glasses and sipped.

"Thank you, Marcus, for such a lovely, and memorable perfect evening."

"My pleasure," Marcus replied and smiled, wishing he could caress her lips with his.

They finished their dessert, and Marcus completed the after dinner ritual of clearing the charges. As they approached the front of the restaurant Marcus noticed the maître d' signal the valet to retrieve his car and ready it for their departure. They passed an older, distinguished looking couple waiting for their seating. Marcus overheard the lady whisper to her husband, "What a striking couple." Marcus glanced into a full-length mirror as he and Theresa paused. They simultaneously noticed themselves standing there together as if it were a photograph of a split-second captured in time. *We are truly a splendid looking couple,* Marcus echoed the thought in his mind. He reached his arm around Theresa's waist and she responded. They stood there holding each other until the valet broke the pose, gesturing toward the awaiting car.

Marcus pulled from the curb, entranced. *This is the Valentine dinner I never had with Anna. It was perfect. Was I foolish to think Anna would be the one? What was it about her, and that situation, that made me want to believe I could will Anna to become the woman of my dreams, when it turned out we were always going in very different directions? She was never going to be that one. In truth, Anna and I never became a couple. We certainly weren't intimately involved. Obviously we liked each other enough to date, but little by little I became less of a priority to her. So Erin was right. Anna just had other expectations for her future, and those did not necessarily include me, as it turned out. I can't feel bad about that. I'm just glad she broke it off, because I might have lingered on until I made both of us miserable.*

And, sweet Jeannie. According to some, I'm the infatuation of a wonderfully talented teenager who has her whole life in front of her. I want to be part of it, but I don't want to confuse her with mixed messages. With Anna out of the picture, I won't be making extra trips to Springfield, so keeping a healthy distance between Jeannie and me should be manageable. Besides, Jeannie has her own mind of what she wants.

The other night when I lay in bed wondering who

would be beside me, I now know that I want it to be The-
resa. But I want to do this right. I know without a doubt
I could wake up with her in the morning, but that would
ruin this perfect evening. That's not who I am and who I
want to be. I want to give her the romance and courtship
she deserves. And that I deserve, too. That might sound
old fashioned to many, but I feel there's something about
the process of falling in love that cements a relationship
and gives it staying power. I'll tell her about Anna but not
tonight. Not on this perfect night.

"You're in another of your trances, aren't you, Marcus," Theresa smiled and reached over touching his hand
resting on the console. "I wonder sometimes, where you
go in that head of yours," she smiled.

"I didn't mean to be rude," Marcus apologized.

"You're not. I just notice you drifting off into Marcus
world, and I wonder what all you have going on in there.
I've studied psychology, you know," she said teasing, "and
I might can help you. I'm very affordable," she laughed
and Marcus with her.

They rode in silence back to her house. Marcus walked
her to the front door and stopped.

"Thank you for a perfect evening. We should have gotten our picture taken," Theresa said.

"I think that image in mirror will stay with me forever," Marcus offered.

"Me too," Theresa reached to hug Marcus.

Marcus kissed Theresa on the cheek, "Good night."
Marcus pulled back, but did not release Theresa. He stood
gazing into her eyes thinking, *I want you. I want you now.*
I can't help wanting to love you, and I don't know why I
haven't seen this all along. But I don't dare. Not tonight.

Theresa came to his rescue, "Will I see you at lunch
tomorrow?"

Marcus released her, recovering from his awkward pause, "For sure. I'll be there," Marcus promised, pulling the glass storm door open for her. Theresa unlocked the front door. Turned and gave Marcus a quick kiss on the cheek, turned and went inside.

Marcus walked down the flagstone walkway of Theresa's vintage home to the sidewalk, then paused and turned halfway around and looked back at the front door. He resisted the urge to race back up the walk, knock on the door, and embrace Theresa passionately when she answered and kiss her with deep reckless abandon. Instead, he got into his car and started the engine.

As he let the car creep into the street from its parking space, Marcus glanced back toward the house where he could see down the side of it. A light came on in the window of what Marcus thought would probably be Theresa's bedroom. He wondered if Theresa, herself, had paused just inside the front door. He imagined her standing there with her hand on the knob, also fighting back the urge to fling open the door and call out to him, "To hell with boundaries, Marcus. I want you tonight." *Naw. That would be too Hollywood,* Marcus smiled to himself and let the car pick up speed.

An intoxicating euphoria infused every cell of Marcus's body. It was as if he and his car levitated instead of rolled through Theresa's neighborhood in route to Riverside Drive that would take him the two-and-a-half miles to his condo.

Marcus reflected back on that Valentine Day dinner with Anna that turned out nothing like he had expected. *I felt sure after four months of dating that Anna was ready to move our relationship along, but man, was I ever wrong. I left disappointed, unsure of myself, and pissed.*

Tonight, I didn't expect to feel this way by the end of dinner. Tonight, I feel like my whole life just changed before my eyes. Did I just fall in love with Theresa during dinner? Or, did I just discover that I've always been in love with her and couldn't see it, or wouldn't see it, because I was so focused on Anna? Regardless, I know I'm on the right track with the right woman, finally.

Tomorrow, maybe at lunch, I'll tell Theresa that Anna and I called things off, and that I want to be with her. There will be no more boundaries between us. I also better let Lauren know that Anna and I are over.

13. New commitment

Marcus lay on his back thinking about the previous evening with Theresa. He rolled his head and looked at the vacant side of the bed and let his mind wander what it would be like for Theresa to occupy that space. The soft features of her face playing peek-a-boo through the undone strands of blonde hair. Marcus imagined caressing the roundness of her shoulders before exploring the curves of her hips. He pulled a pillow close as if he were reaching around her and snuggling her against his body, cupping her with one hand while embracing her with the other arm. Curled into a cocoon, perfectly spooned, his face burrowing deep in that space behind her ear, which a woman never allows to be explored without permission or expectation. Her faint lilac fragrance lingered, and Marcus sniffed the back of his hand and fingers to test whether it was just his imagination. He wanted her, and telling her couldn't wait until noon.

Marcus retrieved his phone from the nightstand and tapped a message while lying on his back, wondering if Theresa were up yet. "buy you breakfast at the café?"

Marcus went into the bathroom and started the shower. He took a moment and looked across the orderly arrangement of his personal grooming items and wondered what it would be like to share this sacred space with a woman. *How did I drift into letting myself become so alone? Every night and every morning I go to bed and wake up by myself. This must change, but not for the sake of change. I want to get this right. Theresa could be that one. I need to know, and I don't want to waste another day.*

When Marcus emerged from his shower, the face of his phone indicated a message waited. Theresa. "love to! 7:15."

"b watching for u" Marcus replied.

Marcus walked through the front door of Johnstone Energy and into the atrium lobby headed toward the Black Gold Café at the far side. About half way across he saw Theresa emerging from the expansive corridor coming from the oil and gas employee parking lot. He paused to wait for her to cross paths just outside the café. He felt the urge to hug her or take her hand, but thought twice. Theresa was dressed in her usual business professional attire, but Marcus could not help imagining her in the after five dress she wore the previous evening.

"Good morning," he said. "How was your evening?" he asked with a boyish grin.

"Fabulous," Theresa answered as she slipped her hand into his, squeezing it once then releasing it, but letting her middle finger trace his palm.

"Shall we?" Marcus smiled and gestured toward the serving line.

Mavis, the legendary manager of the Black Gold was at her usual cashier station, where she had been just about every workday morning since the JEE campus opened. "Good morning Theresa . . . and Marcus," she spied them coming down the line. When they reached her, "Having breakfast together . . . again?" Mavis flashed a grin.

"Yes, ma'am," Theresa answered.

"Anyone ever tell you what a nice looking couple you two make?" Mavis asked.

"Sometimes," Marcus answered.

Mavis leaned toward Theresa, who stood directly in front of her across the counter, and whispered loud enough for Marcus to hear, "You should latch hold of this hunk, you know. He's quite a catch, and I know a good catch when I see one, sweetie," and Mavis glanced at Marcus and nodded. Then to Marcus, "This one's a keeper, my boy. A keeper."

"We'll invite you to the wedding," Marcus teased.

"I better be a bridesmaid," Mavis retorted. "A bridesmaid."

"Have a great day, Mavis," Marcus took his change and followed Theresa.

Theresa led Marcus to a table by the windows, where they often sat. " I had such a wonderful evening last night. Thank you for making it so memorable and special."

"I haven't stopped thinking about what we looked like together in that full length mirror," Marcus replied.

"Me, too," Theresa looked deeply into Marcus's eyes.

"I wanted to see you first thing this morning to tell you something personal that I didn't want to mention last night, because last night was just about you, and only you," Marcus paused, not quite sure how to continue.

"OK," Theresa's pool blue eyes cast a curious glance, inviting him to go on.

"Over the weekend, Anna and I broke off our . . . our relationship." Marcus could see Theresa's pupils dilate at the news. He didn't know if that was a good sign, or not, but he continued, "We admitted that our lives were on completely different paths and getting farther apart. I think I really sensed it back in May, even before Memorial Day. I think I wanted it to be more than it was ever going to be, honestly. And now, I've let go of it, and I'm completely OK with letting her move on," Marcus stopped there to let the news sink in.

"No regrets?" Theresa asked.

"None. None whatsoever. I'm glad I met her and got to know her. And I learned that you can't really move on to another chapter in your life and cling on to the past when it's time to let go, when it's time to change."

"And what do you think that next chapter will be like?" Theresa queried. She had lost interest in her yogurt.

Marcus looked directly into Theresa's eyes and spoke deliberately, "I'm not exactly sure where it will go at this moment, but I know . . . I know without a doubt that I want it to start with you. I see what's here in front of me right now. I love being with you. I look forward to seeing you every day. I know how comfortable I am and how at peace I feel when we are together. When anything happens to me, good or bad, you are the first one I want to tell. I want to have more of that, and I hope I'm right that you want that, too."

Theresa reached across offering her hand, and Marcus took it, "More than you know," she said blinking as the corners of her eyes moistened.

"You can't move on and cling to the past when it's time to let go, when it's time to change."

"One more thing," Marcus continued, "This is kind of delicate. But I just wanted you to know that Anna. Well we never . . . never . . . uh, what's the word . . . consummated our so-called relationship.

Theresa squeezed Marcus's hand tighter, "If there's one thing I know, it's how sincerely you took your relationship with Anna. Believe me, honoring your boundary rule has been taxing for me. No . . . it was excruciating at times. I'm in love with you, Marcus. And now I can say it and act on it."

"I confess that I've had feelings, and thoughts, about being with you over the months, but always suppressed them. But no more. I realized last night during dinner that I am in love with you. I woke up wanting to tell you as soon as possible. I wanted to look into your eyes and tell you that I'm in love with you, and I want to be with you."

"Oh, Marcus, I've dreamed of the day you would say that to me," Theresa dabbed at her eyes with a paper napkin.

"Fitting that I should tell you here in the café where we first met," Marcus looked around the room. "I think this is the very table we sat at the first time." Theresa smiled and nodded. Marcus went on "So, what do we do next?"

"Turn loose, sweetheart, turn loose. Of course, I want to tell everyone I know immediately, but that might be a little over the top," Theresa half-laughed gleefully. "Last night I lay in bed wishing you were there with me. I want to share myself with you, Marcus. It was all I could stand that you would run off to Springfield when I was right here all along. And now, that there's nothing holding us back, I want to relish that moment when we come together with all the delicious anticipation that leads up to it," Theresa said.

"Why, Theresa Younger, you are even more of a romantic than I imagined," Marcus squeezed her hand.

"Hopeless, I'm afraid," Theresa laughed, "and maybe a little old fashioned as well."

"How about we get away for a weekend? Someplace out of the way where we can just be alone and completely with each other. We could leave on a Friday afternoon and come back Sunday night, maybe," Marcus offered.

"Soon?" Theresa inquired with a tone of excitement.

"How about next weekend. Not this one, but the next one?"

"Perfect," Theresa agreed. "This is a big step for us, Marcus, and I want to let it settle in for a few days. I want to allow myself to be deliriously happy. And keep our destination as a surprise until we leave. You know I like surprises."

"OK. I promise it will be a weekend to remember. And when word gets around and it gets back to Mavis, she'll start talking to you about wedding colors," Marcus joked.

"Purple like lilacs," Theresa said, "Lilac purple, when it's time."

* * *

Marcus was on cloud nine all day. At lunch it was difficult treating Theresa like it was business as usual. She crossed her legs under the table and put the instep of her foot against his calf. It felt intimate and private—a completely new sensation to Marcus. The intoxication of this new love completely washed away the sting of Brad's acrid rebuff the previous morning. He could hardly contain his joy, anticipating spending his first evening with

Theresa in her home as her lover in waiting.

Finally, after racing home and changing into something more casual, Marcus stepped up to Theresa's front door. It was open so that he was visible from inside through the glass storm door. Theresa appeared within a few seconds and unlatched the door. She had let her hair down so that its full length brushed the top of her shoulders. She had changed into a pair of shorts and a sleeveless buttoned blouse. She was barefoot.

Theresa locked on to Marcus's eyes as she nudged the door ajar. Marcus caught the door and pulled it fully open. Theresa took a step back, allowing Marcus to enter. She smiled, but said nothing. Marcus silently let the door close behind him and took the two steps required to reach her. Theresa put her arms around Marcus's neck inviting him to gather her into his embrace, all the while never losing eye contact. She lifted her chin and let her lips part slightly and tilted her head to the right as she closed her eyes. Marcus responded by letting his lips find hers and settle in to a slow, lingering kiss. Theresa rose on the tips of her toes to fit the contour of her body to his. Marcus tightened the embrace. She was braless, allowing him to feel the firmness and fullness of her breasts for the first time. He felt himself becoming aroused, causing Theresa to only press herself more closely against him. Their kiss deepened. Her lilac fragrance sweetened the air. Theresa took the back of Marcus's head into her right palm and pressed his face tighter against hers. Marcus felt as if he was being totally consumed by Theresa's caress, and he was perfectly content to dwell there until she relaxed her embrace ever so slightly—a cue that he was now permitted to end the kiss.

Theresa dropped her embrace and let her hands slide

slowly down the back of Marcus's arms taking his hands in hers, "There's a lifetime of where that came from, my sweet Marcus. Welcome home."

"You are my dream come true, Theresa. I'm ready for that lifetime to start," Marcus let her take his hand and lead him toward the den. "I've wanted a home to share with a soul mate. I'm so ready for us to start this life adventure together," he said as they walked.

"An adventure, " Theresa echoed, "That's exactly what I think we will have together."

"So, what's your plan for us tonight?"

"First of all, I want you to find a comfort in being here in this house with me. If it's a place where you feel whole and safe, perhaps, when it's time, we can live here together."

"It's a lovely house, and I really like this area of town," Marcus said.

"I like to say that the houses in this Maple Ridge neighborhood have bones. They seem solid."

"I can hardly wait to take you to my sister's home outside Springfield. Now, that's a place with bones," Marcus emphasized. "And I know my family will take to you immediately."

Theresa led Marcus to the sofa in the den. She sat in the middle and Marcus followed her lead and sat beside her, turning to face her and resting his arm on the back of the sofa. Theresa turned toward him and rested a hand on his thigh.

"I want to hear all about them and hear your stories of growing up with them. That's part of my plan for the next ten days before we go away for our weekend. To spend time talking and just being together and to get comfortable in each other's space. You don't have to entertain me or impress me. Just be here with me. I want us to become intimately familiar with each other's hopes and dreams and likes and dislikes. We'll learn our way of being intimate together as we live together."

"So you won't mind if I take off my shoes too. I'm a barefoot kind of guy as much as possible," Marcus laid his hand on top of Theresa's.

"Absolutely. By all means. Make yourself completely at home. In the meantime, I'll take dinner out of the oven."

"I noticed a yummy aroma when I came in. Smells like lasagna."

"You have a good nose. That's exactly what it is. It's my mother's recipe passed down through her family. I always loved it."

"Do you spend much time in the kitchen?" Marcus asked.

"I've started to since moving to Tulsa. I desperately needed a change of life after the fiasco with Evan and his business. One of those changes has been learning to eat more healthful. How about you?"

"Same as you. I'm not a gourmet cook, but I mess around in the kitchen quite a bit. Healthful eating is important to me since I still fancy myself an athlete."

"I've never been athletic in the traditional sense. I do work out regularly at the fitness club. I take a spin class. I've been thinking about joining a bicycle club."

"That could be fun, and I'd be interested in looking into that," Marcus added excitedly.

"Then don't be surprised with I drag you down to the bicycle shop to get set up with some wheels one day soon," Theresa smiled and giggled as she followed up Marcus's offer.

"I think the adventure is beginning right now," Marcus chuckled.

Theresa leaned forward into Marcus's chest, pulling him to her face, and kissed him softly on the lips. "I love you, Marcus Winn," Theresa whispered after breaking off the kiss.

"I love you, Theresa Younger," Marcus echoed, then added, "And I think I've felt this way since the cookout at Lizzie's. It just feels so good to stop holding back."

The time passed quickly as Marcus and Theresa filled the evening with comparing likes and dislikes. Theresa was surprised to learn that Marcus loved the theatre and the symphony—tastes he acquired growing up the son of a performance artist mother. Marcus was surprised to learn that Theresa was quite the outdoors girl and a bit of a tomboy. She had played softball as a youth, and enjoyed camping on the dozen or so occasions she got to go. And they both loved dogs but had held off adopting one. Perhaps that would change soon, too.

The conversation made the lingering good night kiss even sweeter. Theresa watched from the front door until Marcus drove away. Marcus looked out his rearview mirror and saw the porch light go off. *Interesting how one's life can change so drastically so quickly. Last week at this time I was looking for hope, any hope, that Anna and I would find a way to have a relationship. And tonight? Tonight I know I will have the loving relationship I've wanted and that I'm ready to have with a woman I'm totally in sync with. It turns out that it was Theresa all along. Now, I've got to find the right getaway place that will live up to the importance of that weekend.*

* * *

Marcus could spend every waking hour with Theresa, but he knew keeping his rhythm and balance was important to the way he functioned. There were certain habits he did not want to change, one of them being his regular runs along the river or a jog through the trails of Turkey Mountain. This Wednesday evening it was one of the medium length trails, a little over two miles of uneven terrain. *I hope Theresa and I find a physical activity we could enjoy together. Cycling sounds like a good possibility. I'm looking forward to getting to know all the little things about her that will make us closer. I now know her color is purple. And I know she likes lilac as a fragrance.*

Marcus circled back to his car, retrieved his water bottle and phone and leaned up against the side of the car and tapped Laruen's number.

"Hey, baby brother," Lauren chirped.

"Well, aren't you in a good mood?" Marcus replied.

"Yeah, well I'm a proud momma tonight."

"Why so proud?" Marcus asked.

"Susie just learned today that two of her dance numbers are going to St. Louis to a regional competition over Labor Day."

"That's wonderful. I bet she's excited," Marcus exclaimed.

"Oh, yeah, she's beside herself, so we're making plans to tag along and cheer her and the other girls on."

"Guess the traditional cookout will have to be rescheduled," Marcus offered.

"Looks that way, but there's no reason you couldn't come up if you wanted to, you know, in case you get to see Anna."

"Well, about that, Sis. Anna and I have called things off. Saturday night, actually, after I got back to Tulsa."

"O-o-o-o-h, Marcus, baby, are you OK?" Lauren sounded like a mother fussing over a child's skinned knee.

"Yeah, I'm fine. Disappointed at first, but not surprised, and, truthfully, I've known this was probably coming for a long time. I just haven't talked about it."

"We all thought you two were doing so well together."

"Yeah, but honestly, once Anna got involved with Greer's campaign, we hardly ever talked, and we never spent any quality time together. We intended to, but something always came up. So, I guess, other than being disappointed, there wasn't really that much to lose."

"I remember how excited you were when you met her. What happened?"

"We just finally admitted that our lives were going in very different directions, and we really didn't see a future together. Just that simple in the end," Marcus explained.

"I'm sorry it didn't work out. But there's someone out there for you, I know it," Laruen tried to sound reassuring.

"Actually, Sis, there is someone here in Tulsa I plan to spend time with," Marcus wondered if he should bring Theresa up even as he spoke.

"I hope it's not one of those rebound situations. They don't usually work out so well," Lauren warned.

"Nothing like that," Marcus hastened to add. "Her name is Theresa Younger, and she has been the stand in for Anna on several occasions when Anna stood me up at the last minute. She's an amazing person, and if I hadn't been trying to get something going with Anna, Theresa and I would have already be an item. I just wouldn't let myself go there, but now there's no reason not to."

"I just want you to be happy, Marcus, and if Theresa does that for you she'll be welcome here. Do you have a picture you can send us?"

"I can't say that I do, but we can take care of that soon. You will love her. Everyone does."

"Do you think you should tell Jeannie? You know she's got this thing for you," Lauren cautioned.

"I saw Jeannie Saturday after Greer's rally. Jeannie told me outright that she had more on her mind than me. I don't think Theresa will be a problem."

"Does she know you and Anna have broke up?"

"No. All that happened after I got back to Tulsa, and Anna wasn't mentioned."

"Well, it's one thing for you not to be with Anna any longer and another for you to have already moved on to someone else without Jeannie knowing about it," Lauren observed.

"I really don't get that at all, Sis. Jeannie is always straight with me as far as I can tell, and she told me her focus was school and her new business. I don't think I'm on her radar."

"Just saying, Marcus. Jeannie probably would say that, believing you were interested in Anna. Now, that Anna's out of the picture, Jeannie might have a different idea about things."

"Well, I'm certain of my feelings about Theresa even more than I was about Anna. I've always been proper with Jeannie. I haven't led her on in any way, and I think everything will be fine between us," Marcus asserted.

"I hope you're right about all that. In fact, I expect Jeannie will be on the St. Louis trip with the studio."

"I saw her Saturday because she wanted me to see the pictures she took of the parade. I was impressed. I think she's really in a good place right now with all that," Marcus agreed.

"And, Marcus, you helped her see that she has a lot going for herself. I think that's why she's so infatuated with you. You seem almost larger than life to her right now. She's like one of our family, and we'll keep her close. She has us as well as you, come what may. OK?"

"I'm sure she'll outgrow any infatuation you think she has for me. Let the right guy come her way and she'll forget me like yesterday's left overs,'" Marcus chuckled.

"I hope you're right. Lauren said.

"That seems to happen to me quite a bit," Marcus laughed at himself.

"It sounds like your luck might have changed, if what you say about Theresa is true. I just want you to find your soul mate the way Emily and I have, and I know Mom and Dad do, too."

"Thanks, Sis. There are few things in life I can count on not changing, and my family's love and support is one of them," Marcus found that serious tone coming on. "Hey, I've kept you long enough. Give my love to everyone."

"Love you, baby brother. And send that picture, OK?"

"OK, bye," Marcus hung up.

Marcus and Theresa made no attempt to neither hide nor flaunt their dating. While some of their friends and family might need to ease into the idea of Marcus and Theresa as a couple, Marcus and Theresa needed no such transition.

14. Together

The resurfaced state highway near Eureka Springs became a patchy county road then narrowed into a shoulderless back road that deteriorated with each mile traveled from the main highway. Finally the sign naming the road Marcus sought appeared: Broyles Lane. "Glad we aren't trying to find this in the dark," Marcus signed.

"But it's an adventure. Right?" Theresa teased.

"Glad I printed out a map, 'cause there isn't any cell reception right here for my GPS."

"Well, we wanted someplace out of the way, and I think you accomplished that, Sweetheart."

"Yeah, thanks to Marcy Capshaw's contact list. On a hunch I told her what I was looking for, and why, and a couple of hours later she called back and said it was all arranged and to trust her. So, here we are . . . almost."

"I know it will be perfect. I know our first night really together will be everything I ever dreamed of," Theresa smiled reassuringly.

"Here we go. I think it's the next driveway. Number 5520," Marcus said triumphantly. Marcus babied his 370Z down the gravel driveway. The canopy of trees hid the final destination until he pulled into a clearing that revealed a small, but lush and well manicured lawn and what appeared to be a single level contemporary stone house. A spacious carport extended over the driveway sheltering a parking area of pavers beneath it.

"And this is supposed to be a cabin in the woods?" Theresa's eyes widened with the question.

"Marcy said it was nice and we would love it. She told me where to find the key." Marcus stopped under the carport and turned off the engine. He took Theresa's right hand in his and raised it to his lips and kissed it. "I want to be the kind of man that you will always be proud of. If ever I'm not, I expect you to tell me so I can make what ever changes I need to."

"If I didn't believe that with all my heart and soul, Marcus my love, I wouldn't be here. And I want to be the same for you," Theresa's eyes moistened.

"Let's go in first and check it out, then I'll come out and get the luggage," Marcus suggested.

"Let's," Theresa agreed.

Marcus walked around and opened Theresa's door, a ritual they had settled into every time Marcus drove her. Marcus found the house key exactly where promised. He opened the door, and a flood of light streamed in from a floor to ceiling wall of glass that opened to a deck that ran the full length of the house, presenting an unencumbered vista of Beaver Lake. Marcus and Theresa stopped in their tracks and gasped in unison.

"Marcus, how did you ever?"

"Marcy did it. That's all I know. Honest. Let's look around."

Ground level in front turned out to be the top floor of a three-story house built into the slope of the hill. They entered a great room with sofas and seating areas and a fully stocked wet bar. There appeared to be sleeping quarters on either end of the floor. The next level down housed a kitchen and dining area on one end, the master suite on the other, and a spacious den separating them. A bouquet of roses, a bottle of champagne chilling in a bucket, and two glasses had been positioned on a sofa table to welcome them. Marcus picked up the card next to the roses and read it aloud, "For you, Theresa and Marcus, I wish all the happiness that new found love can bring. Marcy."

"Oh, Marcus, it's perfect, just perfect. I never expected to be treated so lavishly," and with that, Theresa pulled Marcus into her embrace and kissed him hungrily.

The kitchen held other surprises. A note on the countertop explained, "I hope the meals I selected for you meet your approval. You shouldn't have to leave the cottage for anything." Theresa opened the refrigerator door to see each meal properly labeled and ready for final preparation to serve.

"This is absolutely amazing, Sweetheart," Theresa sounded flabbergasted.

"Marcy outdid herself," Marcus agreed. "All we need to add is love," and he took Theresa into his arms and kissed her tenderly.

Each of the three levels opened to a full-length deck through floor-to-ceiling glass walls and sliding doors from each room. The entire house was awash with sunlight and fresh air. After a quick trip through the remaining level, Marcus went to retrieve their luggage from the car.

Upon returning, he found Theresa on the deck outside the master suite. She stood facing the lake. The breeze gently tossed the ends of her hair. As Marcus approached her from the back he caught a whiff of Theresa's lilac fragrance. Without saying a word he brushed her hair to one side and bent over and kissed her on the nape of her neck. She tilted her head slightly and Marcus put his cheek against the temple of her head and, stretching his long muscular arms along side hers, he spread his palms on top of her hands grasping the rails and interlacing his fingers in hers. Theresa pressed herself against Marcus's abdomen and chest causing him to enfold her. Marcus held Theresa silently until she spoke. "Marcus, remember that view from Lizzie's patio? This is almost as spectacular," she said softly and with a sense of awe.

"I was just thinking that. And we have it all to ourselves for the weekend."

"I'm so happy we decided to have our first time together like this." Theresa turned in Marcus's embrace to face him. "Before we go any farther, I'd like a few minutes to freshen up, if you don't mind," Theresa dropped her chin while she spoke and looked up with a teasingly seductive smile.

"While you're doing that, how about I open the champagne?" Marcus suggested.

"I'd like that," Theresa whispered in his ear and kissed Marcus on the side of his neck.

Marcus took his time, mindful that Theresa was preparing herself for the consummation of their love, as was he. *This is one of the most important moments I will ever experience in my life. There is nothing casual or caviler about this for me. I know I am doing this with the intention that I will spend the rest of my life with Theresa. Perhaps, someday, we will have an official ceremony. But for me, for now, this is the moment. What's getting ready to happen between us is a commitment to a lifetime relationship for me. My heart won't let me think of this in any other way. Everything that I was hoping would happen with Anna, and was never going to happen as it turns out, is now happening with Theresa. From the time we met on Valentine Day I sensed a connection with her. She is an affirmation of life for me. My heart leaps in joy every time we touch. I now understand what it means that the two shall become one. Before we fall asleep tonight in each other's arms, our world and our lives will change forever. There is nothing that can undo what we are about to do. There is nothing that can happen that will ever make us any less a part of each other.* Marcus smiled as he thought through the unfolding event and relished the anticipation of it.

Marcus took two flutes of champagne to the bedroom. Theresa was still in the bathroom. Marcus sat the glasses on a side table. He noticed the bed had been turned back. He unbuttoned his shirt and ran his fingers through his hair repositioning some strays. Theresa had insisted he keep his whiskers, and it was taking some getting used to. He heard the bathroom door open and turned picking up the champagne glasses in the same motion.

In all of his fantasies he never imagined how this moment would affect him. Theresa stood in front of him in a white see-through Bardot, off-the-shoulder, babydoll lingerie suspended by two thin straps. It was decorated by a narrow crochet slash that wrapped her shoulders and plunged in the appropriate places to allow her breasts to play peek-a-boo through the veil. The delicate crochet pattern repeated along the bottom hem that graced her hips. Matching lace panties teased at Marcus from behind the veil. Through it Marcus could see the curves of Theresa's full and firm body. She was even more fit than Marcus had imagined. He could feel his pulse in his temples, and he felt the urges rising to possess her. But instead of ravishing her, he handed Theresa a flute of champagne without saying a word. Marcus had prepared a speech attesting his love and intentions, but all that escaped him now. They sipped together while keeping eye contact. Nothing more needed to be spoken.

Theresa took the flute from Marcus and sat it on the dresser. Marcus turned to follow her, but she stopped him with a brush of her fingertips and moved behind him. With the faintest of touches, traced from his shoulders down the length of his arms to his fingertips while pressing her breasts and her left cheek against his back. Marcus took the cue and stood motionless to let Theresa explore at will.

Theresa spread her hands on Marcus's abs, pulling him tightly against her and paused for a moment. After running her fingers up his chest under his open shirt to his neckline, she pulled his shirt backwards off his shoulders and let it drop to the floor. Then, kissing him on the back and shoulder blades, she stroked his chest, eventually finding her way to his waist and let the tips of her fingers explore beneath the belt line. Marcus exhaled, causing his abdomen to collapse and allow Theresa's maiden probe easier access. Marcus started to reach for his belt buckle, but Theresa interrupted, whispering, "Let me." Her warm breath on his back instantly caused every hair on his neck to stand straight. Goosebumps popped on his forearms.

Marcus closed his eyes to heighten the sense of her touch. He tried to breathe deeply and slowly to abate his excitement. Theresa unfastened the belt and unzipped his shorts and slowly worked around the waist of his garments until everything fell to the carpet together. She placed her hands back on his abs and, again, pulled him tightly against her, this time pressing herself firmly against his bare buttocks and held him while she tasted his back and gently stroked his back with her open lips and tongue. The light side-to-side brush of her lingerie against his bare bottom excited him. Goose bumps popped out on his arms, and the back of his neck tingled all the way up to the tips of his ears. And if that wasn't enough Theresa rose on her tiptoes and kissed him at the base of his skull causing him to groan as his knees suddenly weakened and a warmness rushed to the tip of his head.

Theresa allowed Marcus to step out of his shorts, then, put her hands on his hips and with the slightest of pressure signaled him to turn around. Marcus complied. Theresa had taken a step back so that when Marcus fronted her she could lay eyes on him for the first time, head to toe and back again, before smiling and raising her eyebrows in a show of approval. Marcus stood, waiting for the next cue.

Theresa brushed the straps of the lingerie off her shoulders so that the garment slipped to the floor, settling half on top of his shorts, revealing her nude form to Marcus for the first time. She stepped to Marcus and embraced him against her bared breasts and lifted her face inviting him into a lingering and hungry kiss.

Once breaking the kiss, Theresa lifted Marcus's hands to explore her. This time she stood still and let Marcus take his time touching, kissing, and caressing to his heart's content, until finally, as she had done to him, Marcus turned Theresa's back toward himself. He lightly touched the outside of her shoulders, then allowed his fingers, as if they were moving the planchette of a Ouija board to spell out the answer to a cryptic question, travel from the outside of her shoulders across her collar bone to meet at the base of her throat, where they paused before turning down her sternum through the valley of her cleavage to her navel to await further instructions. They came as Marcus kissed Theresa behind the right ear followed by a soft nuzzle. His fingers flattened on her tummy behind the elastic of her panties, then spread. The elastic expanded so that Theresa's lingerie slid willingly over her hips and dropped to her ankles. Marcus allowed his hands to slide around to Theresa's backside and caress the firm roundness of her bottom, as he moved his kiss to behind her left ear. There was nothing Marcus could do to quell or to hide his excitement, nor did he want to. Theresa turned to face him. As he looked intensely into Theresa's eyes he hoped that somehow his thoughts telepathically made their way into her mind, *this is the most whole I have ever felt in my life. I give myself totally and completely to you with all my being.*

Theresa led Marcus to the bed. "I am yours," she whispered and lay on the fresh, soft sheets.

"And I am yours," Marcus whispered as he went to her.

15. New paths

A new normal for Marcus and Theresa flowered overnight into a bond Marcus didn't know could exist between two people. All the sweetness, tenderness, intimacy, and passion he had imagined, and anticipated, for that moment of consummation paled in comparison to the actual tsunami of emotions that swept him into an ocean of joyous exhilaration in which he now blissfully sailed.

The handful of dalliances Marcus had experienced, mostly during his college years, were nowhere in the same emotional universe as what he had first shared with Theresa twelve days earlier in that secluded lakeside cottage on the third Friday of July. When the moment came for them to fully give themselves each to the other, the transformation was surprisingly instantaneous and complete for Marcus. He simply could not imagine himself without Theresa. There would never be another day in his life that Theresa was not part of.

The rest of his life had finally begun.

On this first August morning of the year, a transformed Marcus entered the conference room of the Johnstone Energy's human resource department that doubled as a classroom when needed. A massive floor-to-ceiling whiteboard made up one entire wall that gave the impression of a high key photographic background. It caused Jerry Abernathy, the HR vice president, Nelson Johnstone, and a third person, a woman with her back to Marcus, to pop out in contrast as they stood in conversation. Jerry noticed Marcus immediately as he entered. "Marcus, come in. We were just talking about you." Everyone turned to greet Marcus.

Nelson extended his hand, "I hear you had an interesting trip to Montana."

"Yes, very informative. Thanks for making it happen," Marcus said.

Jerry took over, "Marcus, I want you to meet a new member of our team," referring the young woman. "May I present Dani Novac. Dani is a geologist. Dani, this is Marcus Winn."

"'Marcus extended his hand, "Dani, I think we've met. Didn't we meet at lunch a couple of months ago?"

"At Theresa's table," Dani replied. "It was actually back in mid April."

"That was a crazy time, wasn't it?" Marcus nodded.

"Tell me about it," Nelson agreed with a chuckle. "That's when Marcus, here, first appeared on my radar. We all were going through a bunch of changes at the time." Then Nelson turned to Jerry, "Jerry, why don't we get started?"

Everyone gathered around the conference table, and two other HR staff joined the group. Jerry introduced them as recent additions to the company, Drew and Jessica. They were writers and trainers. "HR is expanding its role to develop and provide leadership courses to our employees. This is a bit of a change for us since we have usually relied on each V-P to bring in whatever training they needed at the time. That was almost completely technical. No leadership or people skills. That's changing with this new initiative. Thanks, Marcus, to your presentation at the retreat."

"I had no idea it would lead to all this," Marcus said humbly.

Nelson interjected, "My daughter, Lizzie, leaned on me hard after Marcus's speech. She's been telling me for years we needed to address the people skills around here. She'd tell me, 'Dad, you've got a lot of smart people working for you who don't know how to play together.'" Nelson chuckled as he spoke, evoking a similar response from Jerry as he nodded and rolled his eyes as if visualizing some of the scenes of personality conflicts he'd witnessed over the years.

Nelson added, "I wanted to make this first meeting to show my commitment to this change, Jerry. I want everyone here at the table to know from me directly that this initiative starts at the top. This whole energy industry is changing. I wanted to bring together both the renewable and the traditional oil and gas sides to make a statement that this is a unified priority for everyone at Johnstone Energy. I think this is the start of something that could improve our culture across the board."

Jerry picked up, "That's why we've added Dani to the team. We thought it was important to roll out this program with two of Johnstone's rising stars, if I may be so bold as to call you both that," he smiled looking at both Marcus and Dani and continued. "You are both young, talented, and highly regarded among your peers and supervisors. We checked you out. We want you to be the faces of this program. You represent the future of this company, this industry, in fact. We wanted a male-female tandem to represent that this program is for everyone." Jerry paused.

Marcus spoke, "I'm excited to be part of this. My only concern is that this might take me away from my duties as a team leader, which is where I feel my priority has to be."

"I know there will be some adjustments, and that's why were going to take the same approach filmmakers use when producing a movie. Jessica, why don't you explain our approach," Jerry motioned to Jessica.

"Drew and I have been working on the content and scripts for each of the segments. We want to use you and Dani as co-hosts at the beginning and end of each segment. We plan to produce all those segments that involve you at the same time, then edit them in," Jessica explained.

Jerry picked up, "So, we won't be continually interrupting your work, but when we do the taping, we will need you for about a week. We've already gotten approval from your supervisors, and they were eager to see you get this opportunity."

"I don't know about Dani, but I've never done anything like this," Marcus said.

"Me neither," Dani confirmed.

"We know some talented production people here in Tulsa. You'll have a coach to help with the on-camera part. Marcus, you know her. Amy Capshaw," Jerry explained.

"If Amy's on the team, I have no reservations whatsoever," Marcus said showing some relief.

"I did one project in college—a documentary on geology with some film students. I did an on-camera interview, but that's all," Dani offered.

"We won't do anything spur of the moment," Drew added. "The production crew likes to have everything scheduled in detail to minimize changes and get the most out of their production resources."

"Plus we're making this a multi-platform program that includes social media, online sessions, and live workshops," Jessica added.

"Wow. This sounds big," Marcus looked at Dani wide-eyed.

"I think it'll be fun. I can hardly wait," Dani said.

"We'll be shooting stills during the filming to build some promotional material, and Beverly Trudeau's communication team will help out with all that," Jerry continued.

Nelson leaned forward, resting his arms on the table interlacing his fingers he looked intently at Dani and Marcus as he spoke, "I think you two are getting the picture of how big this is to Johnstone Energy. I want this to send a clear and unmistakable message about the kind of company we are–a modernizing of our culture and the way we do business. Our slogan is 'ReEnergizing America's future,' as you know, and that slogan has taken on a new meaning for me. It's not just about our energy industry. It's about investing in our new generation of leaders. Marcus, that's you and Dani and others like you coming up in this country.

"When you get to be my age, you start thinking about legacies. Guys like me look back to see what we've done. That's to be expected, I guess. But I look at my family, and I look out across the cafeteria sometimes at the faces and the tables full of both experienced and new talent in the room, and I realize I'm looking in the wrong direction. I want my legacy not to be what I've done, but what I've made possible for your generation to accomplish from here. That's why I think this leadership project is so important. I intend to be very visible promoting it."

Everyone sat silently.

> *"I want this to send a clear and unmistakable message about the kind of company we are—a modernizing of our culture and the way we do business."*
>
> *Nelson Johnstone*
> *Chairman/CEO*
> *Johnstone Energy Enterprises*

"So," Nelson broke silence "I didn't mean to get so heavy, but I'm personally excited about what can happen here. I'll walk the talk. That's the way influence works. It spreads and infuses everything, and before you know it, everything has been affected with a new way. I don't intend to beat anyone over the head with all this. We're just going to start living it and recognizing it in positive ways. Not a program of the month—a new way to lead and live."

Everyone around the table nodded their approval. Nelson continued, "Marcus, you used a word in your speech, which I've watched numerous times, by the way. That word was INPowered. That's what I want for this company. I want it to be an INPowering workplace where we help our associates to become INPowered individuals. Get that right, and I believe there's no limit to the future here."

Marcus responded first, since Nelson had been looking at him most intently as he spoke, "You can count on me, Mr. Johnstone. One-hundred percent."

"Me too," Dani added. "I'm so honored you think

enough of me to ask me to be part of this."

"I know you both are up to this challenge," Nelson said. "When this goes live, your lives are going to change dramatically. All eyes are going to be on you to be the examples of the program you are promoting. That can be a little overwhelming, but from what I know of you two, you can handle it," Nelson paused again then continued, "and with that, I'm going to excuse myself and let you all get some work done."

All rose in unison. Nelson shook hands with everyone and walked toward the door, then paused and turned back to the group starting to retake their seats, "One thing more. In this group, I'm just Nelson. OK?" He smiled that wide Johnstone smile, nodded once, and exited.

"Thank you, Nelson," Jerry acknowledged for the group.

Marcus scooted up to the table, "Nelson sets a high bar, doesn't he?"

"I'm excited. Still, I'm a little nervous about being on public display all the time," Dani confessed.

"Are you having second thoughts, Dani?" Jerry asked.

"No, not that. It just hit me how much is riding on this project, and I don't want to disappoint Nelson or anyone else who recommended me," Dani explained.

Marcus shifted around in his chair to look more directly at Dani, "I went though those same feelings leading up to the leadership retreat. Even though I got a lot of support, I was nervous until I got on stage. Something clicked, and I realized I was enjoying it. I've had to get used to a lot of people around here recognizing me, and I don't have a clue who most of them are. That's kind of a weird feeling. You finally just accept it as you become more comfortable with the change. But it has made me more self-aware of how I present myself," Marcus said.

"Are you still the same person you were a year ago, or do you feel like you are playing a role of some kind?" Dani questioned.

"I know I've changed, but at my core, deep in my heart, I believe I'm the same. If anything, all the attention has made me feel more humble and appreciate what others have done for me. I feel sincere, and I hope I come across that way."

"How have you managed to keep balanced?" Dani continued. The others at the table were now very interested in the conversation she and Marcus were having.

"I've been lucky to know several people at Johnstone who keep me honest. My supervisor, and Elliot Sloan, who everyone here knows has been mentoring me, and of course, Theresa Younger, who daily, keeps me on track," Marcus smiled at the thought of Theresa. "Dani, make sure you have those kind of friends who will tell you the truth you need to hear, but do it kindly."

Dani nodded quietly. Marcus noticed Jessica tapping furiously on her notepad. Everyone else noticed that Marcus noticed, and all eyes shifted to Jessica deeply involved in her note making. Jessica looked up to see all eyes on her, "What?" she looked surprised.

"Influence spreads and infuses everything, and before you know it, everything has been affected with a new way."

"You looked like you were going to poke a whole in that screen," Jerry teased.

"This is good stuff, guys," Jessica exclaimed. "This could be a leadership session by itself. What Marcus and Dani were just talking about, I mean."

"How so?" Jerry was curious.

"This idea of how important it is that leaders surround themselves with people they trust to keep them honest and real. Being able, not only to hear what others are telling them, but building an environment where it's OK for others to speak truth to them," Jessica explained.

"Right," Drew jumped in, "we don't have anything in the training about that. We should definitely work it in," he agreed. Drew continued, "Marcus, we have your video and some notes that were passed on to us from Erin Morales about some of your early ideas. She said they changed how you worked with your team. Is there anything else you've learned recently that you think we should include in the training?"

Marcus had a ready answer, "You just saw Nelson do it right here at this table, and it just now hit me. In fact, I got to meet a congressional candidate over the Fourth weekend who told me that if you aren't creating change, you aren't leading." Marcus noticed Jessica making notes as he spoke again. "Leaders lead others through change. They take the initiative to make things better. They don't wait around for a supervisor to assign them a task when it's obvious something needs to be done."

Jerry added, "It's like the saying that it's easier to get forgiveness than it is to get permission."

"Nelson did something even more basic," Marcus went on. "He's starting a culture change. He wants to create an environment, a culture, where leaders are ex-

> *"INPowered leaders surround themselves with people they trust to keep them honest and real. They build an environment where it's OK to speak the truth."*

pected to also create environments where employees can take more initiative and thrive. No more bossing people around, is the way I heard that."

"Yeah, it becomes the Johnstone way," Jerry said.

"A culture where everyone feels reenergized. Where they can use their individual creative energy to make things better," Dani observed.

"Yeah, Dani, I think that's it," Jerry echoed.

"Wait," Jessica interrupted without looking up, "Not so fast. Say that again Dani, what you just said," Jessica continued her furious note making.

"Uh, OK. Let me see if I can say it the same way," Dani hesitated. "Reenergized. Where everyone can use their individual, or personal, creative energy to make things better."

"That's it," Marcus agreed. "I've seen that at work in my team back when we were putting our funding presentation together. Everyone was involved contributing what they were most energized about, and everything just came together. Plus they all were excited as a group about their results. Nelson told me that was what impressed him most about our presentation. How everyone was in it together, and it was so obvious to him."

"OK," Jerry leaned back in his chair, clasping and rubbing his hands together as he spoke, "We've obviously got some great ideas percolating here. I think this group is going to work well together. Jessica, Drew, how about you take this and work out the details of the modules we are going to develop, and we get this circulated to Marcus and Dani so they can see the bigger picture." All nodded in agreement. "And Dani, how are you feeling about this project?"

"Better now. I'm comfortable that I can be the kind of spokesperson you need. I'm totally in. And Marcus, I know I can count on you for advice since you are a little ahead of me in all this," Dani sounded more sure of herself.

Jerry summarized, "OK, everyone. I think we've got our work cut out for us. Marcus, Dani, thanks for your time. After we get our outline together we'll get it to you. We will probably want to meet after that and talk over where we are. Is that OK with everyone?"

All agreed. Marcus checked his watch. Nearly 11:00 a.m. He reached into his pocket for his phone, which had vibrated during the meeting.

A message from Jeannie. "when r u coming back to Springfield? miss u. Lauren said u and Anna broke up. sorry, but not surprised. when were u going to tell me?

Marcus winced, *Damn. I shouldn't have put this off for so long. And now I'm with Theresa.* He entered his reply, "sorry. been slammed at work. not sure when I'll b back up. Thinking about a road trip to Colorado over Labor Day."

"going to a dance competition in St. Louis then. Susie's group. photography going nuts. making money. yea!!!! check out my website. miss you sooooooo much. please don't forget me."

"I promise. u r unforgettable."

"won't let u forget me, Marcus. will b n touch.

Marcus pocketed his phone and headed back to his lab. *I hope Jeannie isn't angry with me. I need to tell her about Theresa, too. She's right. No reason to keep this from her. I love my new life with Theresa. We're spending almost every night together, and I'm sure it won't be long before we move in together.*

16. The big picture

Congressman Wakefield and Marcus sat in matching leather armchairs directly facing each other. Marcus knew a congressman's time was always at a premium, and he wondered how many others had already occupied his chair that day and what particular business they had with the congressman.

He expected the office to be more adorned with photos showing the congressman with supporters and political personalities, with whom congressmen usually like to be seen. A U.S. flag stood to the right hand side of this desk, and the Oklahoma flag occupied a like position on the left hand side. The flag of the Cherokee Nation stood to the left of the Oklahoma flag. The only photo of any size presented the congressman and his family—wife, son, and a daughter—in a casual setting, wearing matching outfits, and anchored by their golden retriever lying at their feet. *Corny,* Marcus thought. *Bet that one was taken for a political brochure.* A photo of the congressman and President George Bush, the 43rd President, and another photo of him being sworn in at the U.S. Capitol, his wife and children looking on, sat on a side table. The children were much younger in the photo, so Marcus guessed it must have been from his first swearing in ceremony.

Marcus had researched Wakefield online. The congressman had been reelected three times by wide margins and enjoyed a seventy-five percent approval rating in Oklahoma's first congressional district. Before going to congress, Wakefield served one term in the state senate.

He and a college friend had started a recycling business while at Northeastern State University in nearby Tahlequah. The business was still operating and growing— something Wakefield was proud of. He was one-quarter Cherokee and an ardent supporter of Native American values and issues.

Pleasantries aside, Wakefield got to the point, "Marcus, I wanted to have some time privately with you to hear about your experiences in wind energy. There's a lot of interest in it world wide, as you know. But there's also a lot of resistance. Many believe the wind farms are eyesores and have as many negative environmental consequences as positive. How do you answer that criticism?"

"I've heard those criticisms, too," Marcus began. "I'm just an engineer. I haven't got into the politics of renewable energy. On the whole I believe the positives outweigh the negatives. There are issues we have to work out. It will take research into new ways of harnessing wind."

"New ways? What do you mean?" Wakefield asked.

"There is only so much we can do mechanically to improve efficiency regardless of the size of the windmill. We have to get generation closer to users. We might even have to rethink what a windmill is."

"That's interesting. Are you involved in that kind of research?" Wakefield wanted to know.

"No. Millennium operates with current technology invented by someone else. We tweak it to improve efficiency. We're getting about all we can out of the field; so, we're mostly trying to keep everything going," Marcus said, stopping short of saying, "but."

Wakefield picked up on the hesitation, "but?"

"I'm not sure how much I should say. I work for Millennium and we do have some confidentiality rules."

"Rest assured," Wakefield interjected, "I won't discuss anything you say with anyone else. This is strictly for my understanding. I don't expect you to spill any company secrets."

Marcus continued, "What I can say is that I've got some ideas. I don't have the staff or the funds to pursue them within Millennium at this time. R-and-D money would help."

"Aren't there R-and-D programs in the universities?" Wakefield asked.

"Maybe, but I haven't heard of any. University wind energy programs are few and far between, as far as I know," Marcus quickly added, shifting his weight in his chair.

"I've only heard of a couple myself," Wakefield agreed.

"Wind energy is in its infancy. All we've done is try to build a better version of a windmill. And the windmill has been around for over a thousand years," Marcus offered.

"Are you saying you have some innovative ideas, but no way to develop them?" The congressman shifted his weight matching Marcus's posture.

"I think we have to ask different questions about the way we think about wind and how to take advantage of it. And yes, I would like to lead a research team to explore them," Marcus admitted.

"Have you talked to Nelson about your ideas? Nelson is pretty open-minded, from what I know of him."

"No. I haven't brought it up to anyone at Millennium yet." Marcus leaned forward resting his elbows on his knees and interlaced his fingers.

"How far along are you on your ideas?"

"Preliminary. I've made some sketches and done

some crude calculations on whether my ideas might work. Mostly nights and weekend stuff as I've had time."

"What if I could put you in touch with some engineers who might be able to move your ideas along?" Wakefield inquired.

"Well, I'm not far enough along yet, and like a lot of engineers, we are a suspicious group and we keep ideas close to the vest. Self-protection, you know. You started a business, and I'm sure you were a little cautious about who you told at first. Right?"

"Actually, most people thought we were a couple of crazy college kids, which, I think, worked to our advantage. But I can understand your concern, from what I've heard about industrial espionage and competition for commercially viable ideas. Anyway, I haven't really schooled myself on this industry. I'd like to hear why you got interested, and how the industry basically works. Would you mind bringing me up to speed?"

"Sure, I guess so," Marcus agreed. "How much do you want to know? I can get carried away," Marcus grinned.

"I'm honestly in no hurry. I'd like to hear all you can tell me precisely because you don't have a political agenda."

And with that Marcus began with the Oklahoma City tornado of 1999 that got him intrerested and explained wind generated electricity, answering questions from the congressman as he went. Wakefield leaned back in his chair and relaxed. Marcus was impressed with how intently the congressman listened and the depth of his questions and insight.

Then Wakefield surprised Marcus by taking the conversation in a slightly different direction. "I really appreciate your patience with me. I know I'm a novice on this topic. As a congressman I get hit from all sides by special interests wanting legislation that gives them an advantage over competitors. There are multiple sides to the renewable energy arguments. We're facing debates about policies and regulations that will either foster or restrict where the industry goes. A lot of my colleagues have taken hard positions on opposing sides. Right now it could go either way. I want my position on this to be well informed, not propaganda from any one industrial perspective. I also want to create as many possibilities for a reliable and sustainable energy supply that also creates jobs and protects our environment."

"That all sounds good to me. Why is that so difficult?" Marcus asked.

"Vested interest, Marcus. Vested interest and change. Sprinkle in some good old fashioned greed and massive egos and the resources to fund their cause, and the pressure gets intense," the congressman explained.

"I guess I can understand that," Marcus said. "Johnstone is both a successful oil and gas company and an emerging renewable energy company. There is tension between the two, mostly coming from the oil and gas side. I've experienced it personally. Some of them really do think Millennium is trying to replace oil and gas. But even I know any change will take decades. And I suppose we really will run out of oil at some point. Then what?"

"You have a long range view of the situation, Marcus. Most don't. To some, the thought and fear of change is the same as the change itself. The actual future is distant and unformed. The fear is now and concrete to those who are whipping it up—who are fighting the change. And when they have a vested interest in keeping things as they are, when they are in control, they can lay the fear

> ## "To some, the thought and fear of change is the same as the change itself."

on thick. I've learned that people will fight harder to keep from losing something than they will to have something better. All it takes is some vested interest telling people that I'm going to take something away from them, a right or freedom or something, and the fight is on."

"I guess I thought that once you are elected, you were in the driver's seat. I mean, after all, you are a U. S. congressman," Marcus said.

"And I'm proud of that. But the game changes after the election. I was unprepared for—even after being in the state senate—unprepared for the line of vested interest that formed outside my door—everyone wanting something. It's relentless. You know, Marcus, I've been looking forward to this conversation. That's why I scheduled it as my last appointment on a Friday. This is the first conversation I've had that someone wasn't asking me for something, or reminding me that I work for them and they expected me to do something for them, to support a point of view or legislation that would benefit them, often at the expense of someone else. When I tell them I can't go along, they try to threaten me by saying they might support someone else in the next election," Wakefield paused and Marcus sat quietly.

"True, Marcus, I have a vote in the U.S. House of Representatives. There are only 435 of us who vote—and 100 U.S. Senators—who make the decisions about our country. The laws change when a majority of us say they do and the President agrees by signing the bill into law. And within the body–the house–the party politics are so grueling that my leadership, or the leaders of a faction, strong arm me all the time to vote their way, or as one leader told me recently, 'we'll get someone who will.' A direct threat to run someone against me in the primary election," Wakefield caught himself and paused, gazing for a moment toward the ceiling.

"There I go, off on a rant. Sorry. It's precisely because I am the congressman that the pressure is so great. I just let people say what they need to say to get their frustration off their chest since they aren't getting what they want. I want them to know I am willing to listen and do my best to understand their point of view, even if I can't fully go along with their request—or demand, as the case might be."

"I had no idea. How do you cope?" Marcus interjected.

"Most people don't, Marcus. I mean, I didn't realize it was so intense. So when I take a stand on an issue, I want to be sure I know what I'm talking about and that my information is balanced and I can defend it. I want to be able to defuse the fear mongers before they start on me. Change is never easy, especially when people think they have something to lose. So I want to give them something to gain that is real and honest and that I can personally believe in," Wakefield relaxed back in his chair again after gradually leaning into his previous so called rant.

"Recently, over the Fourth, I met a congressional candidate in Springfield who told me that leaders lead. That a leader's job is to give people a vision of a future where they could see themselves happy, safe, and prosperous. I remember that he said, 'Leaders lead change,' and I've found that to be very helpful," Marcus said.

"Are you talking about Eric Greer?" Wakefield asked curiously.

"Yes. Yes. I have a friend working on his campaign, and she invited me to meet him before a rally."

"I know Eric. I met him several years ago as his business was starting to take off. He's a good man. I think he has a political future. But we're on opposite sides of the aisle, although we aren't that far apart philosophically," Wakefield said. "I've coined a term for some of us, want to hear it?"

"Yeah. Sure.'

"I call us ProgressiCons," Wakefield grinned as he said it. "We are that moderate group who could work together if allowed to do so. I'm more conservative than progressive, and Greer is more progressive than conservative, but we agree on a lot of issues, and I think we could really accomplish something. But the atmosphere is so poisoned right now. The only change the leadership

"Change is never easy, especially when people think they have something to lose."

will support is their change, their way, and no other way. And that Collins guy Greer's running against, I have no idea how he got elected last time around. He is a . . . . a, uh . . . ignoramus. And I'll deny I ever said that. But Jeez, you can't even talk to that guy he's so hardcore. One of the true fear mongers that just repeats the bullet points he's given," Wakefield paused, shaking his head in disbelief. "But I could work with Eric. I wish the party labels didn't get in the way."

"Maybe you could be one of those to lead that change," Marcus offered. "You'd have my support."

"Thanks, I appreciate that," Wakefield said. "And, by the way, this part of the conversation is just between you and me, right?"

"Right," Marcus replied. "And all I'm asking for is an open mind to investigate the value of renewable energy and to encourage more engineers to get into the field. Maybe some encouragement for universities to invest in specific degree programs in wind energy."

"That I can do, Marcus," Wakefield said as he stood and offered his hand.

Marcus stood, "I hope I was helpful. I appreciate your thoughts on change. I guess we all wrestle with it in different ways. By the way, can I tell anyone we met?"

"Sure, no problem," Wakefield grinned. "Except, you know, what I said about Collins. That's just between us. OK?"

"No problem."

"I kind of already mentioned it to Nelson. That I had asked you for a meeting. He really thinks a lot of you," Wakefield admitted.

That news warmed Marcus. He smiled, "Nelson has been extremely kind and supportive through all this change."

"Tell you what, Marcus, I'm having a reception tomorrow night at a donor's home in Southern Hills. Why don't you come? I can make that happen, and no one will twist your arm to write a check," Wakefield offered smiling.

"I'd love that," the excited surprise in Marcus's voice showed, then, he thought to ask, "would it be OK to bring my girlfriend?"

"Absolutely. I'll have Valerie get the details to you in the morning. OK?" Wakefield said as he led Marcus to the door and extended his hand as a final gesture.

Marcus glanced at his watch as he left the office, *Wow, that time went by fast. Already 5:30. Did I just get over ninety minutes of the congressman's time? Me? Marcus Winn? And I walked out the door with an invitation to an exclusive reception at a mansion in Southern Hills? Better give Theresa a heads up.* Marcus tapped Theresa's number.

"Hey, lover Wind Boy," Theresa had taken Jim Bob's derision and turned it into a term of endearment, as only she could. Maybe it was the seductive way she could say it. "What time you coming home tonight?"

"I'm running a little late."

"Me, too. Still at work for a few more minutes. Learned that a supervisor doesn't just punch the clock."

"Probably about eight. Still want to get a short run in," Marcus said.

"That'll give me some time to get a little housework done. Don't want you to think I'm a slob."

"I'll bring some dinner in so we won't have to mess up the kitchen. OK?"

"Deal," Theresa said.

"Hey, and there's something else. Guess what we're

doing tomorrow evening?"

"You're whisking me away for a surprise romantic weekend?" Theresa was quick, "Wait. Already done that," she giggled playfully.

"Check," Marcus laughed, "Something different, sort of a social coming out for us," Marcus continued.

"Coming out? Like how?"

"The first time we are seen at a high profile social event introduced as a couple," Marcus said with certainty.

"OK. Now I'm interested. What's the event?"

"A reception for Congressman Wakefield in Southern Hills, guests of the congressman himself," Marcus sounded proud.

Theresa was silent for a couple of seconds. "How did all this come about, my darling Marcus? What have you been keeping from me?" she said in a teasing tone.

"You're the first one to ever know anything about this, except Nelson Johnstone, as I just found out, but I just spent an hour and a half alone with Congressman Wakefield in his office. We met at the retreat back in May and he asked me to meet with him when he came back to Tulsa for the August recess, and that's were I've been."

"And why did he want to meet privately?" Theresa pressed.

"I'll tell you all about it over dinner. But think how cool this is, to be first seen publicly as a couple at such an exclusive event?" Marcus said exuberantly.

"Marcus, you are such a romantic," Theresa teased.

"Hopelessly," Marcus agreed.

17. A new vista

Marcus's favorite place to be was anywhere with Theresa. Today, the third week of September, it was driving along Colorado highway 34 through Rocky Mountain National Park, top down, in a rented Jeep Wrangler. The well-deserved week long vacation capped off a hectic month with Marcus pulling late nights to keep up with his regular work schedule and production requirements of the leadership class.

A full launch after Labor Day turned out to be a bit ambitious. Jerry retooled the roll out to happen in phases. Even the best-intentioned plans can change when the details of production, launch, revisions, and follow up come to light. Nelson remained steadfastly committed to the project. The changes would make it better.

Congressman Wakefield's fundraiser was every bit as much fun as Marcus and Theresa had expected. Lizzie and Travis were there, as were several of the other couples they met at the Memorial Day cookout. Alexis and Eva both were delighted to see Marcus and Theresa officially together as a couple.

"I knew it, I knew it, I knew it," Eva kept repeating when she heard the news, "I could see it plain as day when you two stood there holding hands," Eva went on. "Neil," she said tugging excitedly on her husband's arm, "we've got to throw them a party. We know some couples about your age that would just love to meet you," she beamed at Theresa.

"We'd love to," Theresa eagerly accepted.

"Count us in," Marcus added.

Today, the early-afternoon sun beamed down on them maneuvering the switchbacks along Trail Ridge Road. Each day, Marcus and Theresa left their condo in Breckenridge and headed in a different direction taking in the majesty of the mountains, the grandeur of the forests, and the splendor of the changing foliage, especially the aspen stands. Theresa was as glamorous to Marcus in a flannel shirt and ball cap as she was in an after-five gown. She was more adventurous than he had imagined and delighted in the outdoors. Though not a runner, as he was, Theresa more than held her own on the bike trails around Breckenridge the day before. She wasn't kidding about the spin classes. Everything about her was easy.

The winding highway demanded Marcus's attention, but that didn't keep his mind from wandering over the past six-weeks. *Lauren didn't waste any time telling mom and dad about Theresa. It turned out nice, though. They came to Tulsa over Labor Day to meet her. Everyone else went to St. Louis for Susie's dance competition. Theresa totally wowed them. Dad beamed, and mom whispered, "She's the one, son, no doubt about it," when she said good-bye.*

Jeannie's website looks great. She seems to have taken the news about Theresa in stride; although, she hasn't acted very curious about her. She still texts about once a week, but just to let me know there's more to see in her galleries. I know she's totally involved with her work, and her first college classes started after Labor Day. Don't forget me, Jeannie Irwin.

Whitney's gamble paid off. No problems with the screen shots. In fact, the vendor was so impressed that they contracted with her to develop a series of training videos they could add to their tutorials. That put her on the map with the local owner of her billing company. Way to go, Whitney.

That little talk on change to Pete Olson's company went well—more informal than I expected. They totally got the point about the comfort zone, the stress zone, and conflict. Especially the point that the only world any of us can relate to is the world we build in our own minds, and everyone's world is equally valid and valuable. That's why change is always personal, and often disruptive. When we change our minds about something, we often have to adjust our personal identity somewhat. That can be a big deal and very unsettling. That I know without a doubt.

No further contact from Anna. Some people come into our lives for a while. I'm glad she did, and I wish her all the happiness and success she deserves.

Jim Bob. What a character. Not the hard ass I thought. Just a little rough around the edges. He's got a hard shell, but a soft spot deep down inside, and I got a glimpse of it. I remember Elliot told me months before that Jim Bob is

---

"Change is always personal, and often disruptive. When we change our minds about something, we often have to adjust our personal identity."

---

the kind of friend you'd like to have in a tough spot–like at Outfitters. He surprised me with an invitation to join him and some of his buds for a beer after work. I never breathed a word about his two-stepping. I'm pretty sure he's got a thing for Patti. As my sis, Emily, says, "There's a lid for every pot." Jim Bob says Desiree asked about me a couple of times, but not a peep from him about her coming to my room that night. Guess she never mentioned it, even to Patti, or Jim Bob would have probably found a way to let me know he knows. It's no one's business anyway. I'm sure Jim Bob has told her I'm with Theresa, and she hasn't made any effort to contact me. That seems so long ago. I hope someone sees all the deep beauty that is beneath her surface beauty.

Brad was the big surprise, though. Well, maybe I shouldn't have been too surprised, that he asked Erin for a transfer to another team last week. Never said a word to her about his blow up at me. Just tried to understand where he was coming from. Told her transferring him would be a good change for all concerned. I suggested she consider Sue Ann for Brad's slot. She promised she would.

Sanjar went to Austin over Labor Day to see Angie. He got his first taste of ranching with her brothers. He was saddle sore by the time he got back to Tulsa, and his stories were hilarious. He confessed that his ranching skills were crude, but he dazzled Angie's mom with his swing dancing moves.

Nelson told me how impressed Congressman Wakefield was with our visit. He wants a personal tour at Burns Flat after the November elections. Nelson says there's chatter that Wakefield might run for the U.S. Senate in two years.

"Hey, baby," Theresa put her hand on top of Marcus's thigh, "You're in Marcus world again, aren't you?"

"Guess I wandered off for a second."

"Let's pull over at the next turnout. I'd like to get a few pictures. OK?"

"Sure, the vistas are breath taking, aren't they?"

"I'm going to try to catch it in a panorama. And a selfie to post," Theresa was pleased with her photo-journaling and running account of their trip on Facebook and Instagram. "Even heard from my mom in L.A. She thinks you're a hunk, but thinks you should shave. Doesn't understand how I can put up with the whiskers."

"Hope I get to meet your parents soon."

"They would love you,"

"What does your dad say?"

"He likes the beard. He's happy I found you, and that I'm finally happy. Oh, the realtor texted."

"Yeah, what did she have to say?"

"She said we can rewrite my lease so we can, as she said in legalese, 'cohabitate in the property,' and that the Davenports are open to an offer on the house if we want to make one," *Theresa looks radiantly happy,* Marcus thought.

Marcus pulled over at a turnout overlooking the expansive forest and mountain peaks. Theresa took her photos, and Marcus leaned against the Jeep and pulled Theresa up against him, cuddling her in his arms as they stood looking in silence at the vista. She backed herself deeper into his embrace. *That time I looked out over the breathtaking vista at Lizzie's I felt so off balance. Now, after all the changes this summer, I couldn't feel more solid and connected and sure of myself and where my life is going.*

Marcus nuzzled Theresa below her right ear as he held her from behind. She responded by tilting her head to the left so he could kiss the right side of her neck. He closed his eyes as he breathed her in with a slow, deep draw.

"Ummmmmmmmmmm. You smell delicious," he whispered as he nibbled her earlobe.

A cool burst of mountain air swept through the pass, and life never smelled so sweet.

Theresa turned in Marcus's embrace to face him and gently pulled his face to hers, "You are everything I ever dreamed of. A Prince Charming, a best friend and lover, a man I admire and want to be with forever. My life is finally as it should be, sweet Marcus." Theresa kissed him softly, then, released him. "We better get back on the road."

"Yeah, it's starting to get chilly.'

Marcus helped Theresa into her seat, closed the door, and as he walked around behind the Jeep his phone dinged. A message identified only by a phone number he did not recognize, but the area code he did–Williston, ND.

"Bet you didn't expect to hear from me. I'm coming to Tulsa soon. Maybe Oct 1. Need to see you. Important. Dee."

A lump caught in Marcus's throat, and he felt a knot in the pit of his stomach. An unexplained sense of foreboding surged over him. *Why the contact? Why now? Why the need for a trip to see him? Why important?* He feared that the life he was certain was firmly in his grasp might be on the verge of slipping through his fingers.

THE ONLY CONSTANT IS CHANGE

Discussion section

Change often produces conflict. I define conflict as the state that exists anytime one is not getting what they need, want, or expected, or whenever something is being forced upon someone that they do not want. Change is the process; conflict is often the emotional result.

But not always.

Change is what happens when we solve a problem. An unsatisfactory condition exists. We determine the cause, fix it, and achieve a subsequent state that we hope is more satisfactory and stable. That's a good change, unless our solution causes a new problem for someone else, which sometimes it does. All solutions breed new problems, as engineers often say. And many good intentions produce unintended consequences.

We resolve our conflicts in one of two ways. Either we are able to get what we need, want, or expect, or we come to terms with what we are getting and find a way for it to be OK. In other words, we change our minds about how the situation is affecting us. Another way to say it is we reframe our attitude toward the reality we are experiencing. Both these approaches reestablish comfort in our world.

This episode in Marcus Winn's *Workplace Story of an INPowering Life,* focuses on the issues of Living Change. I have developed scenarios in the plot lines that illustrate personal and workplace change from the individual to the corporate levels. They also illustrate that work life and home life overlap. **In our workplaces, the issue is not how to compartmentalize the demands of living and working, but how to integrate them into a unified whole.**

As in episode one, *Confronting Your Moment of Truth,* when Marcus concluded that everything is personal and we all live in a network of relationships, we find that change is always personal, and our relationships are part and parcel of the change process. As we reflect on this journey into the possibilities from change, we need to prime ourselves with an overview of the underlying dynamics of change. You can refer back to how each scenario in this episode exemplifies various elements of this dynamic.

Everything is personal

The place to begin is understanding that **each and every individual constructs his or her life in exactly the same way.** We all build and protect the comfort zone, which I simply call *my life*. We are the center of our own lives. Everything is about us, and that's all that counts.

We, like all animals, are biologically wired to survive, to procreate, and to protect our offspring. As human beings, we add dimension to our lives through self-consciousness and self-fulfillment: meaning and purpose. We seek to be happy with who we are as a person. Our *self*–identity is bound up in what we believe, the ideals we have, the values by which we live, our family and friends, what we know, the job we have, our interests–all that goes into defining our lives, which is a 24-7-365 project.

As long as all the elements that comprise *my life* are in harmony and none are being threatened, we are in balance–emotional homeostasis. We are in our comfort zone, or comfort world. Life is good.

But when any of these important elements of our comfort are threatened, or we *think* they are being threatened, we enter the stress zone. Like all other animals, we have an *early warning system* that runs deep in the unconscious mind centered in a region of the brain known as the amygdala. Once alerted, this system releases chemicals that give us a feeling that things might not be OK. I use the word *apprehension* to name that feeling. As the threat becomes stronger we grow anxious and the agitation to respond intensifies.

In situations when the amygdala identifies potential imminent, extreme, possibly life threatening danger, everything goes into overdrive, and without conscious thought, we take extreme evasive action to either fight or run. I refer to this as the *panic zone*, a state of extreme reaction devoid of rational thought. All one wants is to regain a state of comfort. While panicking, one is likely to do anything he or she can within their power to escape or defeat the threat. The figure below is my illustration of this conflict progression.

PANIC

Stress

Comfort Zone

© 1990, Garland C. McWatters, Jr

ELEMENTS OF THE CHANGE PROCESS

ORIGINAL STATE
status quo

STABILITY
- Unstable (chaotic)
- Stable (predictable)

STATUS
- Unsatisfactory
- Satisfactory

ISSUE
- Single/isolated/narrow
- Multiple/complex/interactive

SCOPE
- Individual
- Small group
- Large group
- Community
- Enterprise
- National
- Global

INTERVENING AGENT
disruptor

TYPE
- Person
- Nature
- Technology
- Cultural/social
- Authorities
- Institutions

WELCOME
- Unwanted
- Wanted

REACTION-RESULT
- Fight/compete = win/lose/tie
- Acquiesce = surrender
- Resist and manage = cope
- Allow but insulate = coexist
- Encourage but control = cooperate
- Embrace = ally

FORCE
- Weak
- Moderate
- Strong

ALERTNESS
- Unexpected
- Expectred

DURATION
- Immediate
- Years
- Decades
- Centuries

SUBSEQUENT STATE
statum novum

RESULT
- No change
- Worse
- Better

STABILITY
- Unstable (chaotic)
- Stable (predictable)

STATUS
- Unsatisfactory
- Satisfactory

All change must be reduced to the effect on the individual, who reacts based on how the change affects them personally. All effects are relative to the individual. ***Unwanted change is conflict, by definition.***

Phases and elements of change

Heraclitus, an Ephesian philosopher who lived in the 6th century BCE, said, "No man ever steps in the same river twice, for it's not the same river and he's not the same man."

Growth is change. Living is changing. We move from one state to another, often without notice.

We can break the change process into phases and then further segment those phases into the various elements that make up each phase. The chart on the facing page is my attempt to bring to mind some of those elements.

The change narrative sounds like the storyline of a fairy tale. *Once upon a time, each and every day, you go about your life filled with events, people, and routines that make you feel safe, happy, and comfortable. Until one day, something happens to disrupt it all. You become stressed, and you might even panic. You devote your time and energy trying to regain the comfortable life you once knew. Finally, you find a new comfort world that is filled with events, people and routines that make you feel safe, happy, and comfortable. And you live happily ever after . . . until.*

By definition, change happens in the context of time (duration). Change can happen in a nanosecond, or it can take thousands of years. There is an original state and a subsequent state that comes about because of some intervening agent. Usually, change unfolds. That is, change presents itself in a progression of single states that run together in the same way a motion picture is a series of single frames that are presented sequentially fast enough that the brain sees them as a continuous flow.

We can think about the states in certain terms. Is the

state stable or unstable? Is its status satisfactory or not? After a disruptor acts, was there actually a substantive change to the status quo? Was the change for better or worse as far as you are concerned? Did the change affect only one person, or did it involve larger groups or communities? Was the change focused on a single issue or situation, or was it more complex?

We can explore some of the elements of the intervening agent–the disruptor. Was the disruptor an individual, an act of nature, an action taken by a government or other authority? Did new technology come on the scene? Think about the influence of the printing press, steam power, electricity, automobiles, computers, the internet, cell phones. What about social norms and the influence of cultures mixing and mingling?

How did we react to the change agent? Resist, compete, acquiesce, cope, cooperate, ally? Was change expected or a surprise? All these factors play a part in how we respond to the change. The one thing we are doing, however, is trying to be OK with what happens. We, more than anything else, want to get back to a comfortable state where all is well. That's it.

Evolution, Revolution, Transformation

There are three general types of change: evolutionary, revolutionary, transformational.

Evolutionary change is the natural progression of change that happens gradually and often goes unnoticed as it is happening. Examples include aging, ecological shifts, environmental trends, geological changes, and cultural norms. One would expect these changes to occur in the natural course of time.

Revolutionary change comes about through upheaval and causes a dramatic shift or disruption in the status quo. Some examples include war, the sudden introduction of a disruptive technology, business competition, and natural disasters that suddenly reshaped landscapes and habitats. Revolutionary change is often accompanied by turmoil, displacement, or suffering.

Transformational change reshapes someone, something, or a situation into something that is significantly, and perhaps fundamentally, different, and hopefully better. Metamorphosis, conversion, transfigure, and transmute are other ways to describe a transformational change.

Descriptions of the disruptor as a change agent

The disruptor can come in several forms that fit the circumstances of the change. They are kin to the types of change mentioned above; yet, they describe something different about the change process.

Blending or mingling. When two elements combine, blend, or mingle, they can create a third new element or condition that cannot be undone, or return the ingredients to exactly their pre-blended state. For example, when two companies merge to form a new company it is difficult, if not impossible, to reconstitute the two organizations exactly as they were before the merger. Their processes, employees, customers, etc, are mingled to form a new entity. There is an adage that says, "You cannot unring the bell." Blending has that quality to it. Once two or more elements or entities are united, there is no way to revert to the original states.

Friction. When two elements scrape against each other there is friction between them. This friction is disruptive and causes discomfort and/or heat. The results can be combustible or explosive, which might damage or destroy the elements. Just as fire can be both positive or negative, depending on how it is managed, friction can be either good or bad.

Inspiring. The word inspire means to breathe into or to fill using your breath. We experience being inspired when someone fills us with a new idea or message that transforms us in some way, usually for the betterment of others and ourselves. Or we might be inspired by something we experience that becomes a life altering moment. In either event, we are changed by something that comes into us and fills us with a sense of purpose and meaning.

Influence. Influence is subtle. Influence is also a mingling of sorts. Someone enters our world or some event happens and we react to it with subtle and incremental adjustments that we might not notice at first. Attitudes change, norms are redefined, values shift, what was once unacceptable becomes acceptable and vice versa. Sometimes the influence seeps into our lives slowly. Other times it can come about more rapidly. The disruptor sways us to believe and act in ways that we rationalize as necessary and acceptable, even if they are not positive or wholesome.

As you read about Marcus's experiences with change, and all those in Marcus's world who are also experiencing change, review these models and reflect on how your own experiences with change can be better understood. You will be able to process through the change better, and you will be able to benefit from the possibilities that change offers. You also might be able to help someone else through the changes affecting them.

Things change. Change is inevitable. The only question is, will you benefit from it by being able to learn your way through the possibilities arising from it?

Use the discussion questions as a jumping off point to explore the dynamics of Living Change, and all the side issues that arise from it. There are no pat or correct answers–only possibilities for living INPowered.

Chapter discussion questions

I. New heights

1. What does it mean to become disoriented? How can change, even good change, be disorienting?

2. In what way have you ever been disoriented by change?

3. In a period of seven months, Marcus had gone from the verge of losing his job to becoming a company-wide celebrity. Compare and contrast those opposing states according to the elements of the change process model (p 220). What was the intervening agent that instigated the change? Discuss what effect that transition might have had on Marcus. How would such a change affect you, if you were in his place?

4. In what way is a thunderstorm a metaphor for change? In what way is Marcus's desire to transform the destructive forces of nature similar to wanting to channel the negative forces of change into something constructive?

5. Marcus and Theresa were the new arrivals to the group. What made the integration into the group more comfortable for them? How were Marcus's and Theresa's approaches to integrating different?

6. When Theresa talked about the "door of opportunity" being cracked and her tendency to push it open a little and see what happens, what image of Theresa's attitude toward change did that create for you?

2. New connections

1. How is Anna's job a disruptor in Marcus and Anna's developing relationship?

2. What change is Marcus anticipating in his relationship with Jim Bob Danner?

3. What changes in Marcus's role at work are motivating him to reach out to Jim Bob?

4. How does Marcus seek stability in his relationships with Theresa and Anna?

5. What changes are Marcus's friend, Jeannie, experiencing?

6. In what way does Whitney's call represent an additional intervening agent? What shift in states might this represent for Marcus down the road?

7. How did Anna characterize the changes she was dealing with during the conversation with Marcus? How was she seeking stability?

3. No appetite for change

1. What does the setting of Miguel's Taco Café say about the progression of change?

2. Whitney, Thomas, and Ramin all were experiencing changes at work. What was similar and different about their situations?

3. What are some factors that determine whether a state is stable or unstable?

4. Why is slow and easy a better approach to change, as Marcus would have you believe?

5. What do you think about Marcus's comment that people stress out when they are not getting what they need, want, or expected? How is this like being in conflict?

4. Boomtown

1. What change in routine created a conflict for Jim Bob? How would you characterize his attitude toward it and toward Marcus?

2. Why do you think Jim Bob continued to poke at Marcus during the flight? What could he hope to gain from that tactic? If Marcus had gotten into an argument with Jim Bob, how might that have changed the tone of the trip?

3. What did Jim Bob reaveal about his life of change during his rant at Marcus in the truck? How is Jim Bob a product of his response to those changes?

4. What changes have you experienced that caused you to become irritated? What irritated you? How did you respond?

5. Would you describe the changes in Williston as evolutionary, revolutionary, or transformational? Why?

6. If you were a native resident of Williston, how might you have responded to the changes in the community?

7. In what way is Desiree an intervening agent in Marcus's life? How does she disrupt his comfort zone?

8. In what way was Glen a disrupter, and what changes did his intrusion spark between Jim Bob and Marcus?

5. X-factor

1. Marcus experiences a change in his mentor, Elliot Sloan's, reception at their mentoring session. What brought on the change?

2. Discuss how someone who is good at his or her job can be stymied by their reluctance to change.

3. Marcus is concerned that his relationship with Nelson might have unintended consequences. Discuss how improvements in some relationships can cause problems with others. What experience have you had with that situation personally?

4. How did Elliot discuss worker maturity with Marcus that helped him see how he is continuing to evolve in his maturity? What experience have you had with the maturity cycle in your own personal and professional growth?

5. What about those who never quite mature? How do you continue to help them create value in their work experience?

6. Where on the maturity cycle do you think Jim Bob sees the rig crews that Marcus observed? Do you think Marcus would agree with Jim Bob's assessment? Why?

7. Discuss Elliot's concept of the X-factor. Do you agree? Why?

8. How does Elliot use the concept of transformational change?

9. From what you know of Marcus, what transformations do you see going on in his life?

10. What transformations have you experienced in your own personal growth?

6. Risky business

1. How did Marcus show that the comments about the maturity cycle were not lost on him?

2. What was causing Whitney's stress?

3. Whitney said just because someone did a similar job years before does not mean the current job is the same as it was back then. Things change, so the job and its requirements change. What has been your experience with her observation? Do you agree with her?

4. What do you think about Whitney's implication that she wasn't being respected by her managers because of her age? What do you think can overcome any concerns about age?

5. How might the worker maturity cycle help explain what Whitney felt as a young supervisor?

6. How was Whitney already using Marcus's four questions in her approach to the training problem?

7. How does Desiree Chambers continue to be a disrupting agent for Marcus? What Moment of Truth is Marcus facing as a result of meeting Desiree?

7. Independence Day

1. What role do traditions, such as Independence Day parade, play in the stability of a culture?

2. Jeannie is at the parade using her new camera. How does new technology change the way we interact with our surroundings?

3. Lauren mentioned how the chance meetings of Marcus,

Anna, and Jeannie have impacted all of them. What chance encounters have you had that made a big difference in your life?

4. Is it true that some things never change? What does that phrase mean to you? Why is it our perception that some things never change?

5. Jarod and Marcus have different perceptions of how Marcus's life has changed. Jarod cited Marcus's rubbing shoulders with billionaires and jetting around in corporate jets. Marcus had not read that much into those changes. In what ways can we be so close to the change that we don't notice it?

6. Jarod called the stress zone the learning zone. How has that been true for you?

7. What changes did Emily and Owen announce? How will that change impact their lives and lifestyle?

8. In what ways do we voluntarily take on stressful changes and why?

9. What change did Jeannie express at the cookout in her behavior?

8. Getting personal

1. How did Anna's lukewarm response to Marcus at the cookout affect his feelings about their relationship?

2. Why do you think Marcus characterized some of the changes he went through as "brutal"?

3. What's your impression of Marcus's thoughts comparing his reactions to Theresa and Desiree and even his attitude about trying to find the right balanced response toward Jeannie?

4. What kind of change would you say Jeannie is experiencing as her relationship with Marcus's family deepens?

5. What kind of changes must one go through in tragic situations like Christine and her son? How do they find a new comfort world?

6. How did Jeannie's experience with her parent's divorce shape her?

7. What happens when the changes we want don't happen at the pace we prefer?

8. When Marcus asked Jeannie about the way she dressed for the cookout, Jeannie explained she wanted the adults to change their perception of her. When have you consciously changed something about your behavior or manner to affect the way you think others perceive you? How did that work?

9. Jeannie's plans appear to be changing with the new opportunities Ms. Rippetoe is offering. How do new opportunities shape and change our future? What kind of adjustments in plans have you made before brought on by changes in opportunity?

10. Marcus told Jeannie, "Change comes at you from all sides, and it doesn't ask you if it's OK or if you're ready for it." How have you experienced that in your life?

11. Jeannie confessed that her view of changing her life was limited when she first met Marcus. How do we get out of our own mental ruts of what might be possible for us in a different future?

12. What did Marcus say that was so powerful about his experience of giving the speech at Johnstone's leadership retreat that it changed his view of himself?

13. Marcus's family noticed changes in Jeannie's behavior toward Marcus while Marcus did not want to admit they were right. How is it that others notice obvious changes while we remain oblivious?

9. Leaders lead

1. Anna's responsibilities in the Greer campaign seem to be growing. How can changes in job responsibilities change our energy and attitude?

2. How did Marcus's impression of Eric Greer shift as they talked?

3. What did Greer say about the role of politicians in making change happen and how it differed from his current role as a successful businessman?

4. What did Greer claim people wanted in order to make a change?

5. Do you agree with Greer's statement that if a leader is not creating change, he or she is not leading?

6. Greer told Marcus, "people are more afraid of losing something than they are hopeful of gaining something." Would you agree? Offer some examples?

7. Do you agree with Greer's comments about the three types of politicians: panderer, puppet, and pathfinder? Explain.

8. In what category would you place the pathfinder leader: evolutionary, revolutionary, or transformational? Why?

9. What are you picking up from Marcus about his sense of where he stands with Anna and the future of their relationship?

10. What's your reaction to Greer's parting advice to Marcus?

10. Twilight

1. As Marcus heads home from his Fourth of July weekend in Springfield, he reflects that he has changed over the past four days. What have you experienced over a few days that changed you in significant ways so that you could say, as Marcus did, that you were different in some way?

2. Marcus pressed Anna for the conversation about the change he is sensing in their relationship, and it ended with Anna breaking off the relationship. What do you think would have happened if Marcus had not pressed the issue?

3. How had Anna's ideas of what she wanted changed? In what ways was Anna confronting her own moments of truth?

4. What does it say about the need for clarity and changing the direction of one's life?

5. What do you think about Anna's description of conflict and the nature of the conflict state?

6. What is your impression of the way Anna reframed the relationship between her and Marcus?

7. Based on Marcus's earlier reflections about his relationship with Anna, what do you think of his comment that the thought of letting her go was breaking his heart? Do you think he was being honest? Why?

8. What does it take for people to admit that their current path is not getting them where they want to go and to change directions? What have you experienced like that? How did you make the changes necessary to get on another path?

11. Celebrating

1. When people go through emotionally difficult change they sometimes display it in physical changes. What do you make of Marcus's decision to not shave? In what ways have you shown change in your physical appearance or mannerisms?

2. What do you think is better when making a significant change, to ease out of the status quo or to make a clean break and start fresh immediately?

3. How can good news from a friend, such as Theresa's news about her promotion, change one's own feelings?

4. Back at the lab Marcus learned that others were also going through changes. How easy is it to become so preoccupied with our own changes that we are not aware that others are also experiencing changes in their lives? What are some occasions when this has happened to you?

5. Marcus noticed how the team had settled into familiar routines and how they comfortably accepted them as matter-of-fact. What are the pluses and minuses of having these comfortable routines with respect to change?

6. Sue Ann reflected on how good things came from unsettling change around the previous funding scare over their project. What are some good things that have come about from difficult and unsettling changes you have experienced?

7. How does it help a team to know that their leaders also struggle with change?

8. Chris found his work team to be a quasi-support group, and he finally felt comfortable sharing a personally embarrassing situation. What support group do you have that you could go to in times of difficult change?

9. Chris confessed his biggest realization was that he had been living a lie. What was the lie and how had it impacted his behavior and attitude about himself? What similar experiences have you had?

10. What does it say about the health of a team when they are comfortable sharing difficult personal stories?

11. What do you think about Whitney's text to Marcus and her observation that no good deed goes unpunished?

12. When you are trying to make positive changes only to be met with discouragement from others in authority, how do you respond?

13. In what ways might Marcus's relationship and attitude toward Brad change following their conversation after the team meeting?

14. How does Erin's reaction to Marcus's leadership project compare to the reaction Whitney was getting from her supervisor over the changes in technology she was trying to help with?

15. What's your response to Erin's observation that sometimes change finds us and tests us to see what we are made of?

16. In what ways can we be too dismissive of change and fail to grasp its significance?

12. A surprising reflection

1. How does Theresa's attire for their celebration dinner change Marcus's vision of her?

2. How do the renovations in Tulsa's downtown reflect the natural changes in the life cycle of an urban area? How is this analogous to rehabilitating careers and lives?

3. What changes had Theresa experienced that led to her moving to Tulsa? How had she dealt with the personal disappointments she experienced?

4. When we see ourselves in a new context we sense the possibilities of change. How might the reflection of Marcus and Theresa in the mirror affect how he could see himself with Theresa? In what ways do we look in the mirror and see things we want to improve?

5. Sometimes we try to force or will change, but it doesn't work out. Has that happened to you, and what did you do next to either force it or drop it? How did that work for you? Were you satisfied with the results?

6. Marcus experiences an illuminating moment of clarity reflecting on his past with Anna and his future with Theresa. What experiences have you had when you experienced a similar moment of clarity that dramatically affected your life?

13. New commitment

1. If part of affecting change is imagining it, what's the connection between Marcus's imagination of Theresa and his immediate actions?

2. Mavis delivered the second affirmation in less than a day about how Marcus and Theresa looked together as a cou-

ple. What role do affirmations play in generating the energy for making a change? What has been your experience with affirmations affecting your behavior?

3. Why is letting go of the past important to moving on to the future? Why must you move on without regrets?

4. There's a saying that the right things happen at the right time. What's your impression of the timing of Marcus's confession to Theresa that he's in love with her and their decision to move on consummating their relationship within two weeks?

5. Theresa and Marcus take time to get to know each other at a more personal and private level before their planned weekend. What is the importance of transition time in moving from one situation to another? What experiences have you had in which the transition time was important to dealing with a change?

6. Why is transition time necessary and important in making changes that affect other individuals or groups?

7. What did the first kiss between Marcus and Theresa signify about their relationship?

8. What is the value and implications of a new normal?

9. When we go through one change in our lives, how can it affect the rest of our life and the routines we once had? How do we rebalance our life in total when only one aspect of it has been affected?

10. We get so consumed in our own lives and the changes we are going through, that we often overlook the fact that everyone else is living out their life simultaneously with their own changes and adaptations. How does the information Marcus learns from his call to Lauren demonstrate this?

11. When we make adjustments in our life how do we help others get up to speed with how those changes might affect them?

12. Why do changes that seem so life changing for us not have the same emotional impact on others, even our closest friends and family?

13. What do you think about Marcus's strategy for telling Jeannie about his change in relationship status? What if Marcus is misreading Jeannie, and Lauren is right?

14. Together

1. Marcus and Theresa are entering into a relationship that they believe to be permanent. What is the role of ceremony in affirming such dramatic changes in commitment?

2. Why does Marcus value this experience with Theresa differently than his other times with other girlfriends?

3. Marcus was getting used to his beard because Theresa liked it. What changes are we willing to make to please those we love?

4. What kinds of changes are we willing to make in behavior to accommodate others who are significant to us, such as co-workers and superiors?

5. How does fitting into a group affect the changes we are willing to make? What if we refuse to make those changes?

6. Sometimes the actual event is more impactful or less impactful that our anticipation of it. What experiences have you had when the actual impact of an event has either disappointed or far exceeded your expectations?

15. New paths

1. Robert Frost wrote in his legendary poem, *The Road Not Taken,* "way leads on to way, and I doubted that I would ever go back." It speaks to the permanence of some choices. How does this relate to Marcus's perspective of his future with Theresa?

2. Johnstone Energy Enterprises is also in transition. What is Nelson's role in the change process, and what approach is he taking?

3. What does the composition of the HR team developing the leadership program suggest about the types of changes employees can expect at Johnstone Energy Enterprises?

4. In what way was Lizzie Frisk a catalyst for change at JEE?

5. What examples can you think of when an individual had a profound effect on the direction of an organization, a cause, or a community?

6. Change can be planned or random. How is the leadership of Johnstone Energy Enterprises planning the change it wants?

7. What happens when an organization leaves the change that takes place internally up to chance or random influences?

8. Dani and Marcus are being asked to become the face of change at Johnstone. How are they finding their comfort with their new roles?

9. How did Nelson convey his support for the leadership program, and what do you perceive as his expectations of the impact the new direction will have on his company?

10. What might be going through Marcus's mind listening to Nelson and reflecting back on his conversation about sponsors of change with Eric Greer?

11. What is your impression of Nelson's perspective of legacies?

12. What do you think about Nelson's comments about influence?

13. In what way is Marcus being an INPowering leader to Dani?

14. To what does Marcus attribute his ability to maneuver through the changes he has experienced in such a short time?

15. How did Marcus's experience with his project team affirm the INPowering idea that people will respond positively when they are allowed to express their creative energy?

16. The big picture

1. Congressman Wakefield represents another example of change. How do you compare his opportunity as a change sponsor compared to Eric Greer, who is a candidate for the U.S. Congress?

2. When have you found yourself, as Congressman Wakefield, in a situation in which you had to lead a change and wanted to make sure your decision was sound and justifiable? How did you work through that situation?

3. What risk did Congressman Wakefield face in deciding which position he would take on renewable energy?

4. How did Marcus perceive his role as an engineer in the change process of his industry?

5. How does Congressman Wakefield empathize with Marcus's reluctance to share his ideas about new wind energy technology?

6. What do you think about Wakefield's perspective on fear and the reluctance to change?

7. What did Wakefield learn from the changes he experienced from the first time he was elected to public office to his current situation?

8. Discuss the spheres of influence Marcus, Nelson Johnstone, and Congressman Wakefield represent in the changes coming in the energy industry.

17. A new vista

1. What's your observation about Marcus's summation of the changes he has been experiencing for himself and others and the way those changes are playing out? What other changes do you think might be in store in each of those situations?

2. Do you agree with Marcus's thought that making changes personally also requires a change in personal identity? What changes have you gone through that represented some change in your understanding of yourself?

3. What do you think about the idea that no matter how much change has happened, there will always be change, and nothing remains static?